FORM IN CIVILIZATION

'*Remember how much this fine Egyptian work meant. It was not only that so many men were trained to do neat work: they must have had the mind behind the training that could demand it. The demands of each age were its ideals and were the really important things. You may have confidence in the interpretation of mind by the products of art. What, for instance, was there in the writings of the thirteenth century which gave such a perfect picture of the mediaeval mind as Salisbury Cathedral?*'

FLINDERS PETRIE

W. R. LETHABY

FORM IN CIVILIZATION

Collected papers on Art and Labour

With a Foreword by
LEWIS MUMFORD

SECOND EDITION

LONDON
OXFORD UNIVERSITY PRESS
NEW YORK   TORONTO
1957

Oxford University Press, Amen House, London E.C.4

GLASGOW NEW YORK TORONTO MELBOURNE WELLINGTON
BOMBAY CALCUTTA MADRAS KARACHI
CAPE TOWN IBADAN NAIROBI ACCRA SINGAPORE

FIRST PUBLISHED 1922
SECOND EDITION 1957

*Printed in Great Britain
by Butler & Tanner Ltd., Frome and London*

Author's Preface

THESE papers are here reprinted with only minor altera-
tions. Some repetition is almost inevitable in separate
essays on kindred subjects, or different aspects of the
same subject, when they have been written at various
times. The several papers are generally related by being
together an attempt to consider civilization from the
angle of Labour and Art.

1922   W. R. L.

PUBLISHER'S NOTE TO SECOND EDITION

LETHABY's text is given as he printed it in the first edition.
The notes appearing here at the end of the book cover the
few points relating to factual changes since 1922.

1957

Contents

Foreword

THESE collected papers on art and labour, by William Richard Lethaby, first appeared as a book in 1922. Though the earliest paper dates back to 1896, most of the essays belong to the first two decades of the present century. Happily their vitality has not been seriously diminished through the passage of time: on the contrary, the tart and tonic voice of Lethaby, challenging the flaccid aestheticisms of his own time, is more needed to-day than ever. In *Form in Civilization* a robust personality, deeply learned in the arts and vitally concerned with their practice, plays over the whole field. Even if the occasion for some of these essays has passed, partly because of achievements promoted by Lethaby himself, his personal presence on every page will long make this book one to cherish.

To understand the continued importance of these essays, one must understand the movement in which Lethaby had an honoured place as one of the apostolic succession that began with Ruskin and moved on through William Morris. Lethaby was born in 1857 and died in 1931: this made him a close contemporary of Mackintosh and Geddes, of Ashbee and Voysey, and only a little older than Raymond Unwin and Barry Parker. The movement that these men were associated in was known as the Arts and Crafts movement: it started, with Ruskin, as a revolt against the aesthetic hideousness and the moral inhumanity of mechanical industry in its early Victorian manifestations; and it sought to revive arts that were dying and to restore technical processes, associated with handwork, that had been supplanted by the machine. On the surface, the movement was a reaction, for it invoked an idealized image of the mediaeval past, when art and craft and morality and religion were all in the service of a common life. But, at bottom, these leaders aimed at something more central: the restoration of human initiative, the respect for form and quality, the projection of humane ideals of workmanship and beauty. While mechanical invention sought to simplify the processes of production, the Arts and Crafts movement sought to simplify—and amplify—the ends.

This movement, thanks to the work of William Morris and his associates and colleagues, Walter Crane, Cobden Sanderson, Ernest Gimson, William de Morgan, and many others, came to a first full flowering in the eighteen-nineties, though occasional spring blossoms had appeared from the sixties onward. At that time, every aspect of art began to show the effect of the new doctrine: in printing, in furniture making, in weaving, in cottage design, the products of this movement set a new standard, not only for England but for the rest of the world. By this time, the movement had already earned the two great stigmata of success: it was caricatured and it was copied. The caricaturists exaggerated the uncouth and the archaic: the copyists took over the superficial tricks of decoration, particularly the floral forms that were to become rampant

in the Art Nouveau movement. But, for all this, the Arts
and Crafts movement cleansed even the machine arts of
their decorative debasements: it encouraged a taste for
simplicity, directness, honesty, common sense, and in the
end it discouraged historic imitation and empty formalism.

W. R. Lethaby's manhood coincided with this period
of flowering. After studying abroad as a Soane medallist
in 1879, and holding a Pugin studentship in 1881, he
worked in the office of Norman Shaw and had a share in
the design of New Scotland Yard in 1891. In that same
year he began private practice, as the designer of a
country house; and a little later, in 1894, he became
organizer and Principal of the London County Council
Central School of Arts and Crafts. The period from 1894
to 1914 was probably the period of his maximum influence; and, as the papers he published during the first
World War bear witness, the movement that had started
so bravely during the nineties in England had waned
at home whilst it waxed abroad. In the interregnum
between 1910 and 1930, historicism and gentility—vide
the new Regent Street—largely won the day. Though
Lethaby was sometimes inclined to attribute the decline
of the Arts and Crafts to the merciless criticism by the
press reviewers of its exhibitions, more potent social
forces—say rather, more salient social weaknesses—were
probably responsible for this decline.

It would, however, be a misreading of history to describe the decline of the Arts and Crafts movement as
a complete dethronement. Many of the best products of
the twenty years that followed the 1918 armistice, from
workers' housing estates to the posters that made the

London Underground famous, to say nothing of the new stations built for that Underground by Adams, Holden, and Pearson, owe a debt to this movement, and not least to the general broadening of its objectives by Lethaby himself. Lethaby's great importance in the history of British art derived, indeed, mainly from the fact that he carried the Art and Crafts doctrine beyond the stage of pious mediaevalism and blind mechanophobia. Much as he admired Ruskin, he did not think that architecture would be restored to a higher plane by reverting to Lombard Gothic, or to any other historic period; much as he loved Morris, he knew that a folk art could not rest on the kind of slow, laborious craftsmanship that only the rich could now afford to patronize. If, as architectural surveyor and guardian, he loved Westminster Abbey, he could also appreciate, as Morris could not, the cold magnificence of St. Paul's.

Like Geddes, Lethaby was as much at home with science as with art, as ready to use the latest products of the machine as to see that they did not fall short, in their broadened collective application, of the highest specimens of craftsmanship. And again, while Ruskin and Morris were mainly concerned with details, with the elements of furnishing and decoration, with the *stones* of Venice, so to say, rather than with the pattern of the city as a whole, Lethaby beheld all the arts within the context of their civilization, and particularly, as parts of that great common work of art, the Town. 'Towns to live in' is one of the titles of a paper in this book—with the implication that the existing towns of Lethaby's day were, on the whole, fit for anything but the needs of life. And when

he thought of town planning, he thought, with characteristic thoroughness, of every phase of a decent civic life:
not least, the art of cooking. As an example of what *he*
meant by art, he cited the order, construction, beauty,
and efficiency of a naval squadron.

Lethaby's distinction, then, was that he thought of art
as a pervasive expression of the common life. His sense of
life was robust enough to do justice to all its occasions: he
did not disdain the past because he joyfully accepted the
challenge of the present, nor did he undervalue the need
for manual labour and skill because he recognized and
valued the marvellous efficiency of the machine. These
qualities made Lethaby's work and example important in
its own time; and they will keep it sweet for a long time
to come; for our period, though it has advanced far in
many directions, has not escaped from the shams and
fashionable sophistications that Lethaby so heartily
loathed. The shafts that Lethaby directed against academic
art piously copying the past, are equally well-aimed
against the modern academicians, who bow and genuflect
piously, with the same verbal formulae, the same deadly
imitativeness, before the Palladios and Vignolas of the
modern movement, Le Corbusier and Mies van der Rohe.

Lethaby, who was ready to trade all the current art
formulas of the early twentieth century for what he called
an 'efficiency style', would not have been deceived by so
much of what passes for good modern art or modern
architecture to-day: he would have detected the same love
of dead stereotypes, the same bastard taste, the same commercialism, the same fancy packaging under the new
formulas as under the old. He would not have been taken

in, I am sure, by the fashionable mannerisms that produce unliveable houses and flats, unbusinesslike office buildings, and inhuman housing estates. But by the same token, I am sure, he would have admired the factory quarters in the New Towns, the interior of the Festival Hall in London, or the prefabricated schools in Hertfordshire. At almost every point, Lethaby's teachings were at the opposite pole from the doctrines of morals and aesthetics taught by the Cambridge philosopher, Moore, and translated into fashionable aesthetic terms by the Bloomsbury group of the twenties. For Lethaby, 'honest labour hath a lovely face', and no loveliness was worth striving for unless it employed and appealed to the whole man.

The recognition of the part played by the machine in creating new forms has often been mistakenly attributed to Le Corbusier, though the Chicago architects of the nineties, notably Le Baron Jenney, Louis Sullivan, and Frank Lloyd Wright, had already used the machine and formulated its principles in architecture. But certainly no one ever put the case for functionalism better than Lethaby did long before Le Corbusier's manifestoes appeared: all the better because he saw that it was an ordering principle in every aspect of life. There are, as Lethaby pointed out, two contrasting ideals of beauty: a brown-bread and dewy morning ideal and a late champagne supper ideal. 'Who could say', he added, 'which was the right one were it not for Necessity's "You must".' For him, beauty was not something that could be capriciously contrived or rejected: it was rooted in nature, not least in human nature and in the daily tasks of life. But Lethaby has said this in his own words, far better than any paraphrase of mine could say it; and with that I now leave to the contemporary reader this little book, long famous to a secret fraternity of Lethaby admirers.

LEWIS MUMFORD

Amenia, New York
1956

Chapter I

Architecture as Form in Civilization [1]

Towns and Civilization are two words for nearly one thing; the City is the manifestation of the spirit of its population and the larger body it builds for its soul. To build cities and live in them properly is the great business of large associations of men. The outward and the made must always be exact pictures of the mind of the makers. Not only is this so at any given stage, but it is so all the more in a going concern, for the outward is always reacting again on the inward, so that the concrete becomes a mould for the spiritual. Man builds towns so that the towns shall build his sons. As the old Greek said, 'The city teaches the man'.

William Morris says somewhere that the religions of antiquity were the worshipping of cities. It may seem strange, this idea of city worship, but it explains much in the history of art, and we need something of similar sort even now: this and other worships besides and beyond. Before the recognition of the universal and the national we require a much deepened sense of the civic. *Here* comes before the *Beyond*. Almost the greatest question of the time is the one of finding wells for the refreshment of

[1] Reprinted from *The London Mercury*, 1920.

B

our vitality—the fostering of national spirit, town spirit, and home spirit. Such spirit is a very subtle essence, and yet it dwells in houses, and cities are its reservoirs. In the Army it has always been recognized that the foundation of the whole vast violent business is *spirit*. The children of war are wiser than the children of peace. As an example take this scrap from the experience of a new soldier: 'The private is taught from the beginning that the first duty of a soldier is obedience, the second cleanliness, and the third may be gathered from this short dialogue between a drill sergeant and a squad of recruits: "What is the third duty of a soldier?" asks the sergeant. "Honesty, sobriety, and self-respect", we reply. "And what is self-respect?" "Keeping your buttons bright." '

We know that Jerusalem was a sacred city, and so was Athens too in its way. So indeed were all the cities of antiquity, each in its proper status. In the later classical age every one had its impersonation of sculptured image—the *Tyche* of the City. Fragments of a figure of Silchester were found in the Basilica of the old British town; an image which stood for the genius of the place. London and York were also sacred in those Roman days, and the figure on our pennies is a similar Roman imagination for the whole country, *Britannia*. A fine inscription from Ephesus in the Central Hall of the British Museum is a delightful example of the forms and ceremonies observed by the proud cities of antiquity—the ritual prescribed for their worship in fact. This marble slab, about 7 feet by $3\frac{1}{2}$ feet, bears in large clear lettering the copy of a letter addressed by Antoninus Pius to the Magistrates and People of Ephesus *c*. A.D. 140. The emperor approved that the people of Pergamon had written letters to Ephesus correctly addressed with the prescribed titles *First and Greatest Metropolis of Asia*, or the like. He thinks that the people of Smyrna had accidentally omitted this from a decree about joint sacrifice, but they will behave correctly in future, provided that the Ephesians use the approved titles in writing to Smyrna *pre-eminent in beauty* or the like. This is indeed politeness on a high plane.

One of the ways in which civic spirit, pride, and love must be refounded is in the sense of historical continuity. Such a sense of regional reverence is being cultivated in France on a definitely psychological basis, and those alert Americans have already begun to work the ground of their antiquities. A publication of a local historical society, issued as far back as 1900, contains an account of what they in America call 'An Old Ipswich House'. It begins with some words which I must quote: 'The extraordinary production and large circulation of the historical novel is but one of the consequences of the remarkable growth of patriotic societies in this country in the last few years. One of the most admirable results of the movement is the widespread interest in the establishment of local historical societies in the old towns of New England. [Older towns of Old England, please note and copy.] These societies have a very fascinating work before them in the collection of local records, the preservation of old buildings, in the marking of historic sites. This soil is fertile, and delving therein bears rich fruit of interest, love for the community, heightened civic feeling, encouragement of local improvement, and a care for the future of the town. In not a few places the local society has taken some old house for its headquarters, adorning it with attractive historical collections. Such a collection is that of the Bostonian Society, to which the city long ago gave the use of the Old State House.' What might our English towns still do in this way! Or is it to be that for authentic touch with antiquity we shall soon have to go to America? And in passing may I commend this idea to those who have the destruction of the old Dean's House at Wolverhampton in their mind or at least their power?

Germany has long consciously cultivated this field for spirit production, and I remember an official tract on the psychological value of Ancient Monuments in promoting national consciousness. It is in Denmark, however, that an effort to promote national spirit has been most systematically based on a common knowledge of national traditions, arts, and music, and spread by means of their admirable 'Folk Schools'.

Monumental history is a stirring, vital thing: it can be touched. In every town every child-citizen should know the story and antiquities of that place. This has always been the way until now. 'What mean these stones?' the children say, and we answer, 'I don't know'. The history that can be seen and touched is a strong and stimulating soul-food, entirely different from vague and wearying written history.

The historical starting-post is only one of many ways of approach to fine forms of civilization; we must not wait on the order of our going, but go at once and from every point at once. Much is being thought and said about Housing and Town Planning; they are both of the greatest possible importance, but they are not all. We need at least a third to go with them—that is a general cleaning, tidying, and smartening movement, an effort to improve all our public and social arts, from music to cooking and games. Indeed our arts and customs are all indexes and pictures of our inner life. Fine bridges, clean, smiling streets, liberal public buildings are not merely shapes and nothing more. They are essential to our sense of order, brightness, and efficiency, to our pride, confidence, and content. A sore protesting feeling cannot be good for the temper and digestion. A civilized life cannot be lived in undisciplined towns. We must control and tax advertisements to some order, bring pressure on the railway companies to sweep the microbes out of their stations, and we must whitewash our own backyards. The danger is to think of housing and planning as technical matters for experts. It may almost be feared that current talk of town planning and garden cities may harden into a jargon like political formulae.

More and more we become the victims of our words and live frightened by names. Such a name is Architecture. In its mystery vague and vain pretensions may be shrouded, in its shadows hide many minor superstitions about correct design, the right style, true proportions. High priests arise who are supposed to know subtle doctrines and can point the way to aesthetic safety. And yet all the time there are the streets, Edgware Road and Euston Road, Oxford Street and Holborn; there again are our cities, Leeds and Liverpool, Bristol and Plymouth. Surely these patent and indeed blatant facts might raise doubts as to the dogmas. The mystification about 'architecture' has isolated the intimate building art from the common interest and understanding of ordinary men. To talk with a believing architect on his theories is almost as hopeless as to chaff a cardinal. All the ancient arts of men are subject to the diseases of pedantry and punditry—music, painting, poetry all suffer from isolation and professionalism.

Architecture is human skill and feeling shown in the great necessary activity of building. It must be a living, progressive, structural art, always readjusting itself to changing conditions of time and place. If it is true it must ever be new. This, however, not with a willed novelty, which is as bad as, or worse than, trivial antiquarianism, but by response to *force majeure*. The vivid interest and awe with which men look on a ship or an engine, an old cottage or a haystack, come from the sense of their reality. They were shaped so by a higher power than whim, by a higher aim than snobbery. So must it again be with our buildings: they must be founded fast on the rock of necessity.

Wordy claims are often made for 'Architecture' that it is a 'Fine Art', and chief of all the arts. These two claims are indeed incompatible and contradictory. Any mastership in architecture depends on its universality and its service. It is only chief in the sense that he who serves is the greatest. But the 'Fine Arts' are by definition free from conditions of human need, and architecture was specially ruled out from among them by Aristotle. Even so, this idea of fine art unconditioned and free for delight was a heresy of the Hellenistic decline. To Plato and the great masters even the 'musical' arts were to be not only healthy but health-giving; they were to be foods for the soul and not aesthetic raptures and intoxications.

On the other side of the account it may be objected that bare utility and convenience are not enough to form a base for a noble architecture. Of course they are not if 'bare utility' is interpreted in a mean and skimping and profiteering way. All work of man bears the stamp of the spirit with which it was done, but this stamp is not necessarily 'ornament'. The unadorned indeed can never stand as low as that which is falsely adorned in borrowed, brazen bedizenments. High utility and liberal convenience for noble life are enough for architecture. We confuse ourselves with these unreal and destructive oppositions between the serviceable and the aesthetic, between science and art. Consider any of the great forms of life activity—seamanship, farming, housekeeping—can any one say where utility ends and style, order, clearness, precision begin? Up to a point, and indeed a long way on, 'style' is a utility. We have to begin again and look on architecture as an art of service from the communal point of view.

The faces of building which are turned outwards towards the world are obviously of interest to the public, and all citizens have a property in them. The spectator is in fact part owner. No man builds to himself alone. Let the proprietor do as he likes inside his building, for we need not call on him. Bad plays need not be seen, books need not be read, but nothing but blindness or the numbing of our faculty of observation can protect us from buildings in the street. It is to be feared that we are learning to protect ourselves by the habit of not observing, that is by sacrificing a faculty. General interest and intelligent appreciation of public arts are a necessity of civilization. Civic alertness, honest pride, or firm protest are not matters of taste for a few; they are essential activities of the urban mind. In cities buildings take the place of fields, trees, and hedgerows. Buildings are an artificial form of nature. We have a right to consideration and some politeness in buildings. We claim protection from having our faces slapped when we venture into the street. Our cities do not wholly belong to profit-lords, railway companies, and advertisers.

Architecture, however, 'properly understood', not only concerns the man in the street, it comes home to all householders and households. While our eyes have been strained on the vacuity of correct style, the weightier matters of construction and efficiency have necessarily been neglected. We need grates which will warm, floors which may readily be cleaned, and ceilings which do not crack. These and such as these are the terms of the modern architectural problem, and in satisfying them we should find the proper 'style' for to-day. Architecture is a current speech, it is not an art of classical quotation. As it is, it is as much burdened by its tags of rhetoric as Chinese literature. It has become a dead language. The house of the future will be designed as a ship is designed, as an organism which has to function properly in all its parts. Does this not concern every one, not only as economy and comfort, but in the mind? Our houses must be made to fit us like garments and to be larger projections of ourselves. A whole row of ambiguous words, such as design, ornament, style, proportion, have come between us and the immediately given data of architecture. Design is not abstract power exercised by a genius, it is simply the arranging how work shall be well done. The more necessary the work and the more obvious, simple, and sound is the foresight the better the design. It is not a question of captivating paper patterns, it is a question of buildings which will work. Architecture is a pragmatical art. To design in the Classic, Gothic, or Renaissance styles is as absurd as to sculpture in the manner of Praxiteles, paint 'like' Holbein, or write sham Shakespeare. We do not really need a waxwork art by Wardour Street professionals. We require an active art of building which will take its 'style' for granted, as does naval architecture. Modern building must shake itself free from its own withered and cast-off skins.

It is commonly supposed, and architects themselves in older days believed it, that an architect's business was to be an expert in style. Why he should be so was never explained, except, perhaps, by Philibert de l'Orme. According to this authority the Temple of Jerusalem was built in the Classical style, and this work was designed in heaven; therefore this was the only true or revealed style. An excellent argument; modern practitioners have kept up a 'battle of the styles' without any such basis for their logic, or rather their eloquence. But what is or was a style? It is a museum name for a phase of past art. As a means of classifying what is dead and done the style labels are quite useful. It has, however, to be kept in mind that these styles, while they lived and moved, were processes which began, continued, and passed into something else. They were only phases like those of the changing moon.

That which now professes to be designed in a style, or, as the still more disgusting slang runs, to be 'period work', has not the essence of life. It is, therefore, not actually of the style which it simulates but is only in the 'style' of the style.

Indeed, the essence of all the old arts was in their vitality, their response to the natural conditions and the psychology of their times. The better we seem to reproduce their dead images the more we are unlike their soul-selves. There is little more reason for an architect to pretend to work in a style than there is for a chemist. Architects are properly arrangers and directors of certain classes of structures. I would like to say that they were building engineers, were it not that our engineers have failed so shamefully in hiring themselves out for any form of exploitation and in showing no care for order-liness and decency. All the past of architecture, as of engineering and shipbuilding, belongs to us, of course, as race experience, but only as far as the same is true in all fields of science and literature.

Style in a reasonable and universal sense is equivalent rather to 'stylish' than to a style; it interpenetrates the whole texture of a work; it is clearness, effectiveness, mastery, often it is simplification. We have to conceive of it in the building art as we do in literature or athletics. 'The style is the man'—yes, and it is also the thing itself. It is an informing spirit, the spirit of form, it is not a varnish. We have become so accustomed to architecture looking 'dressy' that we have forgotten the logic of clothes and bury buildings good enough in themselves under outgrown rags. It has been a true instinct which calls sham architectural features 'dressings'.

The 'Orders' of architecture are names for particular forms of ancient Greek temple building. Style-names apply to all past fashions of buildings, 'Orders' only to three—Doric, Ionic, and Corinthian. The names are useful as history, but that is all. Now that these Orders have become shop advertisements, even the would-be correct may be more ready to give them up.

Another word which the architecturally superstitious whisper with great awe is 'proportion'. In dealing with such a limited field as the 'Orders', old scholars examined existing examples by measuring them very carefully to find out their proportions; but, if we had them, Greek chairs and tables might be measured in exactly the same way. No general rule of the Greeks has ever been found out by these measurings, and if it had it would prove nothing for us. Proportion, of course, rests properly on function, material, and size. There may be a perfect proportion, for instance, for a certain class of ships, but that will only be discovered experimentally, and not by measuring Greek galleys.

I wish I could find some leverage of argument to bring a sense of citizen responsibility for form in life into the minds and hearts of all, but right and reason are hardly enough. We may, perhaps, hope more in a sense of international rivalry in the works and evidences of life. Civilization is an Olympic contest in the arts and sciences, a sort of international Eisteddfod. It is admitted that we must have literature and we must have music: we must also have building skill, and we have to aim at inducing a flowing tide in all the things of civilization. Of words and arguments I am rather hopeless. One thing only I would

ask of every benevolent reader: that he would take notice
of what he sees in the streets. Do not pass by in a contemplative dream, or suppose that it is an architectural
mystery, but look and judge. Is it tidy, is it civilized, are
these fit works for a proud nation? Look at Trafalgar
Square and Piccadilly Circus, and that terrible junction of
Tottenham Court Road with Oxford Street. Play a new
game of seeing London. We need a movement in the
common mind, a longing to mitigate the vulgarity and
anarchy of our streets and the smothering of the front-
ages with vile advertisements, a desire to clean the streets
better, to gather up littered paper, to renew blistered
plaster. Some order must be brought into the arrangement of the untidy festoons of telegraph and telephone
wires hitched up to chimneys and parapets. These are the
architectural works which are needed as a beginning and a
basis. The idea of beauty, daily-bread beauty, not style
pretences, must be brought back into our life. Every
town should set up an advisory committee on its betterment. We must try to bring back the idea of town
personality and town worship; we must set up ceremonies
and even rituals to bring out a spirit of pride and emulation. If we can only stir up general interest all will yet go
well or at least better. By exalting our towns we should
make a platform for ourselves. As it is, what can great
money fortunes buy beyond swine comfort and titles?
Man is more than a stomach moving about on legs.

A mistake of modern education has been to train for
appreciation of the past rather than for present production. Such merely critical learning comes at last to be
actually sterilizing. As production fails, so even apprecia-

tion decays. Full understanding depends on the power to do. Therefore, leaving the things of the past, press forward to produce, to be, to live. Remember Lot's wife. There is much talk of patriotism, but patriotism requires a ground on which to subsist; it must be based on love of home, love of city, and love of country. Let nothing deceive us, civilization produces form, and where noble form is attained there is civilization. Life is a process, a flow of being, and where there is this vital activity music, drama, and the arts are necessarily thrown off. Living art comes on a tide of creative intelligence.

Chapter II

Town Tidying [1]

I WONDER whether any of us have ever been troubled by the question as to whether art was a serious vocation for a serious life. We have perhaps got into the way of looking on art as a rather remote ornament to life—concert-room music, exhibition-room paintings, and perhaps some special Arts and Crafts. Properly, however, art is all worthy productive work; and, looked at in this way, it seems to me that art is about the most serious thing there can be: certainly it is a very serious thing for us at this time, for our towns have been long neglected.

One of the most seeing things ever said, to my mind, was the remark of Victor Hugo that books would kill art. We understand and believe what we are told in print, but we see very little directly with our eyes. That is, I suppose, why we employ curious people called art critics, who profess to do the looking for us and tell us about it—the blind reporting to the one-eyed. I wonder whether it seems an extreme thing to say that we have partly lost the use of our eyes; if, however, it were not so, I cannot think that we could endure the general disorder in our towns with the advertisement-plastered stations

[1] Arts and Crafts Society, 1916.

and paper-littered streets: the general dreariness, dullness, and nothing-to-be-doneness except to get away in a fast motor-car.

Much study and research have been devoted to the great question of town improvement from the point of view of planning of late years; but it is not of these technical or architechnical matters I want to speak. I want to speak of what should be the concern of ordinary people—all of us—with the common problem of life in towns.

By thinking of art as a special matter dealt with by special people called architects and painters and musicians, we have gone far to banish beauty from our towns and our lives. What I mean by art, then, is not the affair of a few but of everybody. It is order, tidiness, the right way of making things and the right way of doing things, especially the public things of our towns and cities. It is a question of pleasant railway stations, of street cleaning, of controlling advertisements, of making our houses fit for sane people to live in, and of cooking meals fit for healthy people to eat. Moreover, it is a question of keeping our heads up in civilization. We have not been properly led about these things; we have not been properly taught. If we were alone in the world it might not so much matter; but we are not alone, and it is a tremendous question this of keeping up fine quality in our work, in our towns, and in our lives.

The need for public art not as superabundance of luxury, but as an absolutely necessary part of the ordinary life of people in communities, has really become for us a very pressing question, and I want to impress it on your minds by repetition. I would have it taught in schools. I would have it become the chief question at elections, so that even members of Parliament would have to show some interest in the beauty of the towns they are supposed to represent; and now it strikes me they do 'represent' them very perfectly. I would have all art societies join in some common bond for common work for life's sake outside the professional grind and their trade union points of view. Directly I speak of art in the town it will be natural for you to think of a picture gallery or a special statue or some 'art lamp-post', or other over-ornamented object; but I must again insist that is not what I mean. I mean the making of our towns fair and fit to live in from end to end, the whitewashing of back courts, the laying down of turf, the reducing of the advertisement mania, the smartening of the railway station, the seeing to it that there shall be some place in every town where decent food can be got comparable to what one gets abroad, the provision of some space of clean country where one may take a dog for a walk without shame. We need to make it an enthusiasm, a game, a 'movement'—a tide of tidying.

Think of any country towns you know in detail, begin with the railway station, or rather two miles before the station, where the miserable advertisements of Mr. X, the ready-made clothes man, and of Messrs. Y, the furnishers on the hire system, begin. Then look at the slatternly shanty called the station and the mean station road. Towns are not necessarily like that. Towns should be made to house a proud and intelligent race of people, and we have to see to it that they are thought of and dealt with from that point of view. We must aim at having the best towns in the world, each with some decent unspoilt country around it, and each with sufficient internal means of civilization from music to pots and pans. We must be given more to be proud of: do not our leaders know that pride is strength? I dare not let myself describe our towns as they are; but I am anxious to recall them to your own minds; and even when you leave here may I beg of you to look at Piccadilly, which is about the most famous street in England, and then at the next Tube station you come to? Well, they are not good enough! For the earlier part of my life I was quieted by being told that ours was the richest country in the world, until I woke up to know that what I meant by riches was learning and beauty, and music and art, coffee and omelettes; perhaps in the coming days of poverty we may get more of these.

As an example of what I mean by art where order, construction, beauty, and efficiency are all one, may I instance the Navy? We must not be content until our railways are as ship-shape as a squadron. What other arts have we that hold the same beauty of efficiency, carried forward in an unconsciously developing tradition? Just two or three occur to me. Simple, well-off housekeeping in the country, with tea in the garden; Boy-scouting, and tennis in flannels. These four seem to me our best forms of modern civilization, and must serve as examples of the sort of spirit in which town improvement must be under-taken. Everybody must be interested, and it must be half drill and half game. I am here to beg you all to play this best of games—town-tidying.

c

Chapter III

Towns to Live In [1]

WHEN classes of things and groups of activities
have once received distinctive names we are
apt to think of them as special subjects which
can be understood only by few people. Science, Philosophy, Art, Music, Architecture have all in this way been
isolated from everyday existence. Art, in the common
view of it, has been narrowed into a matter of pictures,
especially 'oil paintings' which are brought together in
annual exhibitions, and explained, or at least written
about and about, by people called 'art critics'. The once
flowing stream of Music in a similar way has been turned
into the dry bed of concert-halls, where it is tasted by
other sets of critics. The arts are thus thought of as
specimens you occasionally see in galleries for a shilling;
they have ceased to be a daily inspiration for life. Most
people have come to suppose that they are mysteries
altogether outside the common round, 'not for the likes
of them'; and indeed the arts have been imprisoned by
dealers. We all have to exist, however, and we have to
make up our own minds on hundreds of problems without expert knowledge. As we are concerned with politics,

[1] From the *Hibbert Journal*, 1918.

with manners, and with religion, so we necessarily deal with art in all work, recreation, clothing, cooking, gardening, and indeed, in a word, in living.

This Art about which such elevated yet confusing things may be said when it is considered at its remoter end as genius, emotion, and poetry, at its nearer end is just good workmanship, quality, skill, fitness, rightness in all things done and made. A town, then, is a work of art according to its quality as a dwelling-place for men. Its art is its service and stimulus to life. Some little confusion may arise because we judge beauty quickly by the outward show, and many an old town which we call beautiful may have been neglected into dirt and disease. The dirt and disease, however, do not make the beauty, and during the ages it has been the estimate of life value which has formed and conditioned our thoughts about beauty. Beauty is the evidence of Vitality—the smile of Health.

Without attempting to describe our towns as they now are, it will be admitted that they are not the perfect homes of a stout and proud people at the centre of a great commonwealth. We need not worry ourselves about beauty for a long while yet; there are many prior questions of decency, cleanliness, order, fitness. Our towns have not been thought of enough as organisms and wholes: wonderful work has been done in them in departments, especially in remedial ways, but not so much in constructive ways. The town itself is hardly ever thought of as a cradle of life, a school of manners, and the foundation of civilization. We have accepted our institutions as matters of course, and the problem of intense training for quality in community life has hardly ever been considered. Our better-educated people, indeed, had come too much to look on our towns as places for labour—labour of others—while they could go 'abroad' for recreation. We have to reorganize all our towns as places in which to live and to train strong and willing children. A man is the child of his city, and if he cannot reverence her he is much of an orphan. Even an apostle felt a satisfaction in belonging to no mean city. National spirit and 'patriotism' cannot begin high in the air with flag-waving; they must be reared on affection for home, pride in our town, and the sense of community.

Town improvement is likely to be put aside as some great thing, and doubtless great things are needed; but it is also a common and immediate necessity. Greater things, indeed, can only be satisfactorily dealt with as the result of constant desire and effort. Without experience in the little things grandiose doings are likely to be unrelated and artificial, or even destructive. Many of the smaller things do not raise the question of cost; they are rather matters of custom and training, and much of the humblest kind needs everywhere to be done for the preservation of a minimum standard of order.

In every town there is at least one building for which the Government is responsible, the Post Office; and this fortunately has no unworthy associations. The central authorities should be expected to make the Post Office a reasonable standard of dignity in building and of pleasant orderliness in administration. Here too it would be possible by some finely designed coat-of-arms—which would be next to costless, as it might be repeated by thousands—

to bring in a little colour and special character in a significant way. Most of our people have probably never seen the national coat-of-arms except as hideously engraved and attached to some advertisement. One coloured example in a town would even be educational, and school children might be stirred to ask about the lions of Richard of England and Alexander of Scotland, and the pretty harp. Is not one of the secrets of education to create curiosity?

A more difficult service to deal with, as being neither public nor private, and as being of the utmost importance to the town while not of it, is the local railway system. The municipalities will have at some time to reconsider their rights against the great external exploiting corporations, and require that some proprieties are observed in the stations, approaches, and bridges. The stations especially have been allowed to run down by degrees to a level which is intolerable, and most of them seem to be looked on as mere hoardings for advertisements. We must first of all try to see them as they are, and not go on supposing that stations are 'like that'. This is no question of taste: it is a tremendous matter of national efficiency and discipline. The riot of advertising along the approaches to our towns will have to be controlled into some order, and the citizen must to some extent be protected. Violent advertisement is a form of assault which seeks to gain attention by slapping you in the face.

The town buildings—Guildhall, Market, Schools, Infirmary, Museum—even if they are not yet fine in themselves, should have the distinction of being well kept, tidy, clean, and even smart; they should be good-example buildings. Lamp-posts, tramway-standards, ventilators, shelters, and such things can only be properly designed from the point of view of being perfectly fit for their purpose and unobtrusive; we often make the mistake of forcing them into a bad prominence by loading them with repulsive ornaments. The movable services, like fire-engines and tramcars, which are commonly considered only from the point of view of efficiency, plus a workmanlike smartness, are usually well designed and decently kept, while the fixed ones are often perfect models of fussy incompetence and mistaken compromise. Iron bridges and railway sheds should be designed as a ship is, and then be kept ship-shape. Structural ironwork for supports and railings should generally be painted one of the many tints of neutral grey. The prevalent frowsy red is nearly the worst of all colours, as being irritating. Our great mistake is to make minor things furiously 'ornamental' to begin with, and then to let them decline into slatternly misery. There is no need that our most practical daily utilities should be made repulsive as a sacrifice to what is supposed to be Art: poor Art! what crimes are committed in thy name!

As soon as greater interest in town life can be aroused, improvements must be undertaken in every direction. The smoke nuisance must be reduced, rivers and streams must be cleansed, refuse must be better dealt with, house fronts must be repaired and repainted, backyards must be whitewashed and front gardens planted. The space in front of the town railway station must be made orderly. In foreign cities even the strip between tram-lines is at times laid with trimly kept turf. We need more opportunities to get wholesome food outdoors; indeed, cooking generally might well be made a matter of municipal concern. All the minor items connected with town administration are worthy of attention. The town arms—not the public-house sign—might be redrawn by one of our competent heraldic draughtsmen, and a town monogram could be devised; the street names might be done in better, clearer lettering; and municipal printing can be improved for all purposes.

We have become so subject to words, that arguments to the eyes are little appreciated. The first need is to see with our eyes, for if people only saw things there is no reason why a great change might not soon be brought about. Some reasonable teaching about quality in work— that is, art—has to be brought into all our education, from the Infant School to Oxford; and in every university the civic arts should form an important group of subjects.

We have to set up ambitions for great things in civilization, and induce a flowing tide of high types of production. Interest should be created in every town's story—every town is a Zion and has had its prophets. This town spirit is best stirred by the sight of some older buildings, and such buildings should be preserved as assets for life. Buildings like Cheetham College, Manchester, the Dean's House at Wolverhampton, and even the comparatively modern but fine Town Hall at Birmingham, have a worth which is incommensurable by site value. Civic missions, study circles, bands of hope, and exhibitions are required. Probably nothing better could be thought of, as likely to bring new interest to our towns, than some form of annual festival like the Welsh Eisteddfod. This is not a vain survival of playing at being Druids, but music, the arts, and athletics are all stimulated at those gatherings. Such festivals have been general in all times and countries, and the people are starved for the lack of them. A better organizing of town games should lead to the provision of a proper stadium where athletics would merge naturally into discipline. Local ability should be brought out by the employment of local artists and craftsmen, and towns should compete in civilization as Florence, Siena, and Venice competed.

In every considerable town there is already a building called the School of Art, but it is too much of a watertight compartment, and usually it is allowed little influence. Such schools might be made vital centres for civilization, and even for commerce, for commerce too will fail without ideas and initiative. These schools must become producing workshops; they might as a beginning be encouraged to experiment with derelict industries like Spitalfields silk-weaving. The old special town crafts like Bristol glass, Sheffield plate, Worcester china are of very great importance every way. Some of our museums and picture-galleries also seem to be arranged and conducted as sacrifices to custom without any one clearly knowing what they are all about. Local history and interests should be a special concern, and the School of Art might help by getting together a collection of drawings and photographs of the antiquities of the town and district. The contents should be arranged in the most exquisite order, and so far as possible interest should be renewed by some changes brought about by borrowing and the temporary formation of special groups. In some foreign galleries bowls of flowers are set about. The buildings should be direct, perfectly finished, and even overlighted. Far too many of them were spoilt before the foundations were put in by worry about style and the decision to load them with fortieth-rate ornament, so called. This same is true of most of our buildings; we have indeed been betrayed by the mysterious word Architecture away from reality into a realm of pretence about styles and orders and proportions and periods and conception and composition. If we had had no other word than *building* we might have been living in sound, water-tight, well-lighted dwellings. As it is, it takes an expert student a lifetime to find out that there is nothing in it all beyond the human spirit working on data as presented by custom and common sense. All this aesthetic talk, however, has isolated art from common sympathy and understanding, and no art can flourish in a vacuum. If the people cared we might have noble schools of building, painting, and music in a genera- tion. Everything indeed depends on caring enough, and anything could be condensed from that infinite nebulosity the possible. Glorious new worlds are even now waiting to be born and projected on their orbits, if only we would care and will and work. Great art of all kinds is produced only by common effort over a long time.

Public memorials might more often take the form of works of communal value. Our towns, it must be said, are ill supplied with suitable buildings, from worthy bridges to meeting-halls, baths, drill-halls, and markets. If statues are desired, it must be seen to that they have some 'life-enhancing' quality which is the soul of art. A dull presentment of even a hero only adds to routine and social slumber. Variations of existing types might often give some depth of content; Alfred Stevens's 'Valour' and 'Courage', hidden away in St. Paul's, might lend their vitality to scores of other works. A town impersonation like the Paris 'Strasburg' may be moving if it is done with dignity: all depends on that. Even a big bold lion would be impressive. Where funds are small it is wise to spend them on one thing. A great unhewn stone from the nearest source, with just a name and a date in good lettering, would be far more appealing than a monument of the same cost where most of the money has been spent in bringing marble from Italy and granite from Aberdeen, and the rest has been expended in chipping and polishing these into the necropolis mode. The only way, however, in which a successful monument of any sort is likely to be obtained is to ask some one who can best be trusted to get it done; many of our public works have died of too much committee before they were properly begun.

About a century and a half since there was a general movement towards some ideal of communal culture in our towns, and even small ones had 'Assembly Rooms' erected which for a time became centres of local life. Then came the time of Institutes and Lecture Societies, many of which still do excellent work. A century ago Edinburgh and Dublin were true capitals; towns like York had society; Bath was about the most beautiful modern city in Europe; Brighton, Leamington, Tunbridge Wells, Buxton, and Cheltenham had style; and many of the seaside places, like Hastings and Weymouth, were truly beautiful. Oxford was as lovely as anything in the world; and old prints show that most of our towns were beautiful as a matter of course—ugliness, and especially vulgarity, had not been invented. In all the larger places forms of fine craftsmanship were in daily practice—good cabinet-work, clock-making, and so on; the shop-keepers were little merchants. Norwich was an excellent school of painting; Newcastle was the best school of wood-engraving in the world.

Without bringing a railing accusation against the works of the nineteenth century, we may all agree that town development was a little one-sided, and that plenty has been left for us to do. The quick growth outran strength and sense of fitness and order. The railways attacked towns rather than served them. However, the first works of the great expansion were in many places carefully constructed. Brunel did not foresee all that the engineers of the next two generations would hire themselves out to do.

Around our towns we must preserve or redeem a space of pleasant suburb not too remote, a wood, or common, or 'walk', or 'view'. The planning and planting of our town parks and gardens are frequently done according to a dry and harsh ideal. There is too much gravel and iron railings; they must be made less like cemeteries and more like gardens simple and sweet. We too often spend our efforts to produce added weariness. We lay out sham splendours of cracked cement and cast-iron around a fountain which holds no water, rather than get a carpenter to set up a strong home-made seat by a space of clean turf or a blossoming tree.

Poetry and Art come from insight into the essentials of

things and life. Our refounding of these and a national
school of Music must begin with the simple and the
obvious; we must try to construct a ladder of salvation.
Our towns have to be made delightful homes to live in,
rather than delightful to get away from.

Chapter IV

Housing and Furnishing [1]

THERE is much talk of Housing at the present time, valuable and necessary talk, but yet up to the present it is a case of much talk and little house. Still it is necessary to try to stir up general interest, even enthusiasm and passion, in the hope that a real beginning may soon be made.

Housing, of course, is not merely a cottage question; it is an immense national question and also an immediately individual question in which we should all be decidedly interested. Housing is health and temper and a large part of living. It must be one of a very few greatest of all questions. Pride of home is pride of country. Housing is the necessary preliminary 'plant' and 'capital' for our national life. We have to accumulate force for renewal. We need to clear our general aims and to consider our policy as a whole. Our aim should be to develop a fine tradition of living in houses. It is a matter for experiment, like flying. We should seek to improve in detail point by point. There are enough sketch designs; now we want solids. Exquisite living on a small scale is the ideal. 'House-like' should express as much as 'ship-shape'. Our

[1] *The Athenaeum*, 1920.

airplanes and motors and even bicycles are in their way perfect. We need to bring this ambition for perfect solutions into housing of all sorts and scales.

The chief obstruction to our having better houses has been the superstition that they should be built in a style. There is a great difference between being built in an imitative style, Elizabethan, Jacobean, or Georgian, and being built *with style*. A motor-car is built with thought for 'style', that is finish and elegance, but it is not built to look like a sedan chair or a stage coach. To be concerned with style imitations and what the Americans call period design is not only irrational in itself, but it blocks the way to any possibility of true development. If you have your eye on *that* you can't see *this*. To go on building houses in the cocked-hat and brass-candlestick style is not only rather imbecile play-acting, but it destroys rational growth. We have to put an *efficiency style* in the place of this trivial, sketchy picturesqueness. Even leaving out the style trimmings would be something. If you cut away disease and surplusage, you strengthen and consolidate. There are many cases in which the half is greater than the whole. We have to prune our building forms as we prune a fruit-tree and sternly cut away the dead wood. Whenever we concentrate on some directing datum, some reality like health, serviceableness or even perfect cheapness, true style will certainly arise as the expression of this and the other human qualities embodied. To design in 'a style' is to design a seeming which stands in the place of style proper. This style superstition is a much greater evil than I could persuade you to believe. It filters down to lower and lower strata, and the poor man is at last persuaded that nightmares of vulgarity and discomfort are necessary offerings to 'style'.

The dwelling-house should be sound, dry, light, warm, and sweet. We should save in all thoughtless extravagances, and concentrate on the conquest of dirt, disorder, and waste. Houses must be built for living rather than for letting. A false and confusing opposition between science and art has been allowed to arise, and indeed is rather fostered by expert simulators who 'go in for old-world effects'; but properly there is no strife between science and art in architecture. It does not matter a bit if we call flying an art or a science: the art of house-building is practically one with the science of housing. If we must worry over strict definitions, 'science' may stand for codified preliminary knowledge, and 'art' for operative skill, experiment, and adventure. Science is what you know; art is what you do. The best art is founded on the best science in every given matter. The art of shipbuilding is the science of shipbuilding in operation. The notion that there are special 'art forms' or 'art colours' has led to all sorts of pretences and sham picturesquenesses. Art is high competence in doing what is worthy to be done. Very occasionally there is in art a sort of poetry over and above: such addition of feeling can be expressed by giving it an *h* and calling it *heart*.

Soundness and convenience, light and heat are the great essentials in house-building. In planning a house there are two main requirements which are to some extent in opposition and must be compromised in various ways: the needs for sunlight and for compactness. The difference between a sunlit room and one that is not so blessed is so great that it cannot be measured. To get sun in every room, some spreading of the south front is desirable, but much can be done by projections and bay windows. On the other hand, a square unbroken plan is the most economical and conserves heat. Four straight walls will enclose the greatest space when they form an exact square, and all ins and outs are costly in respect to walls. Again, simple roofs are less expensive and much sounder than complicated ones. A too 'picturesque' roof will certainly become a leak in your income. Fireplaces should be put in the internal walls to keep the heat in the house.

Other things being equal, so far as may be, preference should be given to local materials and to traditional ways of using them. This traditional use is embodied experience. On the other hand, we should beware of supposing that any reasonable materials such as concrete, cast-iron or plastering are necessarily inartistic. It is the business of art to use the materials given to us by Nature so that they will look well; and when they are well used they will look well. For example, there seems to be an assumption that Welsh slating is inartistic; but this can only be the effect on us of the dreary rows of little speculative red-brick houses which we have seen that have such roofs or rather lids. If the houses ceased to be dreary the slates would soon look quite another colour. Some slight modification showing that there had been care for good work would at once make a difference; and at last they might glow with the light of heaven. Concrete should be frankly used. If blocks are better for constructive reasons than a continuous mass, then use blocks by all means, but do not imitate stone. The surfaces should be finished with white or colour wash.

Frankness is the great thing; disguises and subterfuge are always repulsive in building. Bungling, pretence, and compromise are the enemies to be feared.

Our best English house-building is probably the best in the world, and the experiments of the last two generations have brought back into use many valuable ways of doing things. Our need now, however, is to consolidate and *perfect*. The several units have to be improved one at a time. Plaster ceilings are too much given to cracking and even to falling; under the doors there are draughts; there are too many dirt traps; fireplaces waste heat. Further, there is unnecessary expenditure in 'features' which nobody cares for—'handsome' cornices and bold skirtings. A wood picture-rail a foot or two below the ceiling would usually be far better than the futile cornice, and a small hard wood strip might often take the place of the skirting with advantage. We are given over to mouldings; the plainer and smaller, but of better quality, are to be preferred to 'handsome' and poor. Doors are often made unnecessarily large and windows undesirably small; then pipes are hidden away and put where they freeze. We must aim at getting the small house as perfect as the bicycle.

Besides the problem of building new cottages there is the very serious problem of repairing old ones. To destroy all the old cottages of the land which are not up to a living standard would so alter our countryside and villages that much of England would be destroyed with them—the 'Old England' we talk about so plentifully.

D

To destroy these cottages would be like a preliminary step to asphalting the country all over. These dear cottages vary from district to district as the soil varies—they are dialects of building, and hold history and emotions which we cannot plan and specify and contract for. Of timber, stone, flint, granite, cob, brick; roofed with thatch, tiles, and stone slabs, they grew out of the ground and are as natural as rabbits' burrows and birds' nests—they are men's nests. Yet the aggregate number of the unfit must be enormous, for they have been terribly let down and each one is a special problem.

Most of them, I am confident, could be mended by reasonable expenditure if we cared to care for them. What is needed is that the various local authorities should at once consider and set about experimenting. Putting in concrete floors, lining the damp walls and relaying the roofs would often do all that is required without any injury to the old buildings which show that the British people had grandfathers. I may say here that I believe that the Society for the Protection of Ancient Buildings are giving attention to this tremendously urgent matter, and I know that from their long experience in caring for old and frail buildings their help would be worth having.

If our old British cottages could be made strong, and to look as if they were honourably guarded, then there would be an incalculable value over and above so many habitable houses. There would be a gift included of strength and pride for all of us. I remember reading many years ago a German government report on the psychological value of the old buildings of the country in forming the German spirit. Almost more than anything else the old cottages represent England. Old is old, and new is new; don't destroy the one nor make the other sham antique.

The great snares in house furnishing are: extravagant expenditure on the worthless; the lowering of our demands to a penny picture-postcard level; overcrowding with trivialities, and worse. Often these household gods are really devils undisguised. Housekeeping should be a struggle for quality. A room, like a garden, can only be kept in order by continual weeding. There are two main data, affection and efficiency. If there is any pot or pan you really love, go on keeping it till you don't, but make up your mind. As Morris put it, 'keep nothing you do not know to be useful or believe to be beautiful'. The recent over-use of the words 'art' and 'artistic' has led to some insincerities, and at this time it would be better, I think, to aim at being *scientific* in both our house-building and furnishing. Beware of much ornament, especially of the machine-made sort. Merely routine ornament is quite a disease, a surface eruption which is often repulsive.

Another point: the buying of old furniture, the pawn-shop ideal of furnishing, has been overdone; it has encouraged dealing and discouraged making. A fine piece of old furniture is, of course, a delightful possession if you have it, or if it 'comes to you', but the right thing now must certainly be the encouragement of living makers; further, you will thus escape the danger of buying sham antiques. Some time ago I saw in a shop a carved chest labelled 'saved from Ypres' and all scorched by fire. It had been made antique with a sandblast, and burned by a lamp.

Some admirable experiments in the making of cottage furniture are being made at the L.C.C. Furniture School in Shoreditch. For small rooms it is desirable to get things for corner positions, where they are more out of the way.

The first aim in decoration should be to brighten and stimulate. Decoration which adds to gloom would be better undone. As decoration is something beyond utility, it should be good of its kind, and a little that is good goes a long way. Not only is one good picture worth a thousand bad ones, but *they* are a positive balance on the wrong side. Aim at quality, at cheerfulness and brightness. The use of much white is not merely a fad; a white room is much lighter than if otherwise coloured, and it looks larger. I should like to have two rooms arranged at an exhibition, one with whitened walls and a few averagely good things, the other covered with a deep crimson paper and other objects 'to match'. Every one would, I believe, feel the stimulus of the former. It is sometimes argued that dark tints don't show the inevitable dirt, but to make a thing dirty all over so that it shall not show more dirt is doubtful policy. A not too dirty fair room looks cleaner than a new gloomy one.

Do not allow any blue to be put into white for ceilings, rather a touch of yellow to make it slightly creamy. Greys, buffs, and fair yellows (not hot) are all good for painting; also some greens, but these require judgement. Black occasionally, as in skirtings, is sharp and clean without being frowsy. Arrangements of any two of these are likely to be pretty safe. In the case of painted chimney-pieces and the like it is good policy to paint the flat of the shelf red or black—just the flat without any thickness.

The edges of doors might very well be painted in the same way differently from the surfaces. Graining of wood-work might now be brought back if the graining was not imitative but frankly ornamental, and not in berry browns but in simple gay colours. Wall-papers should be fair in colour, with the pattern distributed all over and not in bunches. Beware of all extremes like the Viennese black-and-white chequers lately so much in vogue. Beware, too, of purple—a mourning colour. Distemper washes are good, and some of them take varnish very well and make an excellent surface. There is a custom of hanging pictures too high; if they are not good enough to be seen, banish them still further. Finally, I would suggest that enough is not now made of our Schools of Art. Picked students should be employed in decorating houses with interesting personal work if they would take an oath to be simple, sane, and sweet, and not acid, frantic, and sad.

Chapter V

Design and Industry [1]

D URING the last two generations several attempts
were made in England to deal with the changing
conditions of production in respect to design and
machine industry. Other efforts of the same kind are
demanded at the present time in view of the fact that
foreign competitors have taken over our ideas, have more
fully exploited them and then have turned them back on
ourselves.

One of the first serious attempts to bring design and
modern industry together was the great Exhibition of
1851. The establishment of the Royal College of Art and
the Victoria and Albert Museum set up types of institutions which have since been copied all over the world.

The Arts and Crafts movement of the last quarter of
the nineteenth century was also a specially English pro-
duct which has been much studied and imitated abroad,
while it has been allowed to struggle hopelessly at home.
With occasional extravagance and affectation it is certain
that it produced ideas in plenty, ideas which, in many
cases, have been taken up and worked by our foreign
rivals.

Design and Industries Association, 1915.

The difficulty has been that the designer and the manufacturer have so largely remained in separate compartments, and that the purchasing public had yet a third point of view. The political economist has preferred to dwell in another watertight compartment. As Adam Smith did not bother about design, why should *he*? He has, in fact, become an idealist of crude labour because he can deal with it mathematically. Quality, he finds, is a disturbing matter of opinion, so he tries to get rid of it by acting as if it were not there.

The Press critic, on the other hand, seems to be concerned only with the qualities which interest him personally just at the moment, and he probably does not realize that he may be killing potential English industries by a hasty word.

It has been extremely unfortunate that the Arts and Crafts movement in England coincided in time with the violent fashion for antiques of every kind. Every one with any pretensions to taste has tried to find Chippendale chairs, 'Adam' book-cases, and other old furnishings. And this has resulted in a sort of curiosity shop ideal which has gone very far toward destroying the higher forms of invention in our household requirements. This, for instance, is the kind of question which our political economists ought to have explained to us if they had not been dwelling apart in realms of ideal abstraction.

It appears that when thousands of pounds are commonly paid for tapestries and curious Chinese pots only low commercial prices will be available for modern efforts. The relations between 'dealing' and production are too complex to follow here, however, and the question must be referred to the critics and economists.

What is needed at the present time is the gathering together of all the several interests concerned with industrial production into a closer association; an association of manufacturers, designers, distributors, economists, and critics. It is therefore proposed to found a Design and Industries Association which shall aim at such closer contact between the several branches of production and distribution, and at the same time explain its aims and ideals, as far as may be, to the public. We ought to obtain far greater results from our own originality and initiative than we have done in the past. We must learn to see the value of our own ideas before they are reflected back on us from the Continent. English designers, for example, set the type of furniture which, especially in hotel furnishings, has spread all over Europe. The English book, from the letterpress to the binding, has very greatly influenced foreign productions. Pattern designing of all kinds for textiles and wall-papers has also been remarkably developed here, and the English fashion in design has led the world during the last generation. Nearly all that was wanted was confidence in our powers, faith in our own wares, and the ambition to make as attractive as may be even the cheapest class of goods. The things of which we have been speaking have been produced in England by a special class of enthusiasts for a small number of connoisseurs, and the large manufacturer has not seen what great possibilities there were in adapting these experiments to the larger world of machine industry. Now this is just what our foreign competitors have done.

Design is too often thought of as an inexplicable mystery, and it is difficult to get it understood that design does not necessarily mean a pattern drawn on paper, nor does it involve some strange originality; but it should be just the appropriate shaping and finish for the thing required. Compare, for instance, a modern electric pendant with its agony of contortion, many dust traps, and little brittle leaves, with the perfection of simplicity of an old Dutch chandelier. In the latter the question of originality was never raised; it was made by a process of adaptation and improvement. In much the same way many of our own products of a century ago, Sheffield plate, steel fire-grates, brass fenders, copper coal-scuttles, pottery and textiles, were all admirable; they were none of them frantic attempts at originality, nor were they exercises in some style of the past, Gothic or Louis Seize. They were beautiful because of their fitness and finish.

It is necessary that we should come to closer terms with design in all our industries, yet it is hardly a paradox to say that we think too much about it, puzzle over the questions involved, and offer frantic solutions rather than serene and confident ones. Design is not some curious contortion of form, or some super-added atrocity, but it should rather be conceived of as the fitting of means to ends in the production of works which are good each in their own order. The manufacturer must often puzzle over what will sell, and indeed it must be a maddening problem; but let him rather recast the question into 'What is good, what is the best that can be done for a given price?' and the question of design will at once be simpli-fied if not solved. Is there any guarantee, indeed, that the good thing will sell better than the pretentious bad thing? Probably not, so far as novelty is the chief reason for the demand; but surely the good thing has a lasting power— the best bicycle at a given price is the one which is likely to be selling best. Now if we could produce the best finished metal bed, the best tightly fitting, non-dust holding bookcase, the best and most effective coal-box, all at low average prices, is there not a probability that they would sell like the best cheap bicycle? A good idea in any of these things would be quite a valuable property. Such a bed or bookcase should be improved in its details as the bicycle has been improved; frequently too little thought is given to the books or to ways for conveniently holding them, and too much ill-directed effort is devoted to what has been supposed to be 'design'.

In Germany an immense success has been obtained in the production of efficient hotel furniture by considering the real elements of the problem and paring away extraneous excrescences. The ideas in many cases were borrowed from our own Arts and Crafts Exhibitions, and it may be recommended to some cabinet maker in a large way to try what he can do with an 'Efficiency Style' as a variant to the Early English, Jacobean, and Queen Anne modes.

At least one furniture firm might find its account in perfectly adjusted mechanical fitness. They need not all supply all the styles, and there must be many purchasers who realize that they don't live in Jacobean houses or wear cocked hats.

Efficiency, it will be said, is not all. What is the next step in design? The next step is best thought of as still more beautiful finish, trimness, smartness, brightness.

Then if the thing is in the hands of a real master designer, some little embroidery, as it were, on the plain garment, some little added fun of workmanship, may be permitted, and this is ornamentation. The use of the word at once brings in confusion, especially as the point which is being urged is that seven-eighths of design for industry should be directed towards efficiency.

There is undoubtedly some misconception as to what English people want. There is a large section at least which wants what it can't get. Quite remarkably beautiful cotton stuffs woven with coloured stripes, tartans, and chequer patterns are produced for the Indian market. They would make delightful curtains in country houses, but they are entirely unknown in England.

These are cheap things, but it is also certain that many expensive things will sell if they are only good enough, and such goodness involves design; for example, German publishers have found that a class of illustrated book *must* sell if it is only good and costly enough; there is a limited but almost certain number of art libraries, over Europe and America, which must buy every book of the sort which is produced.

It is obvious that the great prizes of manufacture will be found in ideas and design. Raw material and labour are common charges, and particular methods of production are not likely to make much difference. With a specialty, or an attractive design, the situation changes.

We have so far made an altogether inadequate use of our trained designers. Where they have been employed it has often been too much in the use of paste and scissors, or as drawing clerks making timid variations. Their status is that of humble draughtsmen, not of *experts* who might confer great benefits and receive considerable rewards. We must bring new Chippendales, Flaxmans, and Cranes into our industrial commerce. There can be no doubt that able designers can be provided in England so as to supply any demands which can be made on them. German industrial design, as has already been said, has been founded on a minute study of the English Arts and Crafts movement, and special English advice and designs have often been made use of. The great German type-founding industry, for instance, has been based on a study of the experiments of Wm. Morris, Emery Walker and T. J. Cobden-Sanderson, and the writing of Edward Johnston.

It happens that here in England for two generations men have been spontaneously turning towards the making of things. Morris himself was one of the first educated men who felt this impetus, and he has been followed by hundreds of others, many of whom have made great sacrifices for the crafts in the endeavour to make reasonable and beautiful objects. They have set to work to learn as book-binders, printers, metal workers, potters, cabinet makers, wood carvers, stained glass workers, and the rest, and much truly beautiful work has been produced in this way. Again and again remarkable results have been attained, Mr. William De Morgan's faience is an example. But in far too few cases could the strain be borne, and the results have been all but lost not only to the valiant experimenter but to England. The students in our design schools feel the same impulse towards making things, and show an aptitude which seems to come from this instinct towards workmanship. There is indeed enough designing ability in the country to improve our wares up to any conceivable pitch of excellence, and with due encouragement to bring new life of many kinds into all sorts of industries. Of course any young designer is not likely to know all about a new business in the first month, and he will make mistakes and failures; a percentage for unsuccessful experiments should be written off; but still it must be true that the prizes will go to those who take the risk of employing the best obtainable talent—at least our competitors have proceeded on that assumption.

Chapter VI

Memorials of the Fallen: Service or Sacrifice? [1]

THE other day I was asked some questions on the cost of stained glass, as it was proposed to put a stained-glass window as a memorial in a village Wesleyan chapel. Another memorial has been mentioned to me: 'the form decided on is the replica of some old village cross'; and yet another was to be a 'runic cross'. The spirit of the inquiries was entirely wholesome and sweet, but it raised (as it will in the minds of crotchety people, 'who never agree with what they don't propose themselves') a whole flight of preliminary questions and doubts as to ultimate possibilities. There are thousands of other cases where like questions are being asked without our being ready with considered replies. As usual it will be muddle. Again the generous people are untaught; again they are to sacrifice before an idol, or a whole row of idols.

Is it necessary, is it what the fallen themselves would have wished, that four and a half years of war and destruction shall be followed by a great outpouring of unproductive, and indeed futile, labour? Must a sort of murder be followed by a sort of suicide?

[1] *Hibbert Journal*, 1919.

The problem as a whole in its great mass needs thinking over and out, and it would be well if the intelligent people of the universities, churches, and councils would consider it and take the responsibility of giving some teaching. Have the universities no national functions? It seems that millions of pounds are again to be wasted, and at such a time, in doing what we at most can least well do. Sometimes, indeed and alas! it may be spent in further vulgarizing our ancient churches. Meanwhile Englishmen and heroes have too few houses to live in, and too little vital and reproductive work to do. Why should it be unmonumental to provide some of these? Billiard-marking and diamond-cutting will not be enough to employ all who come back. Would it not be possible to direct some of the memorial streams to irrigating truly productive work? The best of all memorials would be those which helped speedily to organize the drifting masses of men who are returning to *promises*, and the unproductive monuments will not do that.

There is a feeling in the air that we ought to offer pure sacrifice for the fallen, and that there is some meanness in making memorials serve a useful purpose—that we must advertise our regret and compassion in lavish oblations of marble, brass, and glass. Then there are artists and firms all ready to provide the expected right things; but we must remember that these are the priests who live by the sacrifices, 'thrusting their forks into the cauldron'. It is in the nature of things that artists should be chiefly interested in their own matters, and we can hardly expect a general theory from them unless they were called together in consultation, when they would be quite equal to giving disinterested advice. What we most need is some such calling together for discussion. If we could hold a meeting of the fallen and put some suggestions before them, is it the brass and glass that they would choose? We might readily find out with a high degree of probability by holding a meeting of the maimed and injured and asking them what their fallen comrades would have liked—this or that?

The idea of a stone sacrifice is very largely a modern development. Of course there have 'always' been monumental memorials, but they were generally direct records, a writing on a wall, or they were tombs. Now, tombs in antiquity were not simply monuments to the dead; they were eternal houses for those who were in some ghostly way living another kind of life. They were not mere memory memorials.

More self-conscious memorial monuments and pompous tombs came in with the Hellenistic decline. The great 'Mausoleum' of the semi-oriental satrap was soon followed by huge trophy monuments, triumphal arches, and sculptured memorial pillars. All these are heathen, imperial, and part of the apparatus of hypnotism by pomp.

On the other hand, great and serious works of service have generally been associated with the thought of memorial purpose. It was known that only life can ensure further life: only living grain can fructify.

Pericles rebuilt the sacred high city of Athens as a memorial of the Persian War. Alexander founded Alexandria as a memorial to himself. St. Sophia, Constantinople, was in some degree a memorial of the putting down of the Nika riots. So our own wise Alfred re-founded London after withstanding the Danes. Most of the great works of men have been memorials, and all the greatest memorials have been aids to life. The earliest churches were martyr memorials.

In the Middle Ages the favourite memorial was abbey founding, and abbeys were experiments in community life. At the Renaissance time colleges, schools, almshouses were built. 'Almshouses': the very words are memorially beautiful if we had not starved the meaning, so thin, bony and grim—cold as charity. Of modern-time works Waterloo Bridge is very far the finest memorial we have; indeed, it is in a different category from 'memorials proper', and is in its way perfect. Again, the Albert Hall is as much better than the Albert Memorial as it is more serviceable. Trafalgar Square is at least superior to the Nelson Column. Only reality can give the true monumental note.

If we think again of our need and purpose, there is an enormous volume of noble constructive work which is necessary to the life of the people, works from those of a national scale down to those suitable for our villages.

The nation might consider some such schemes as the following:—

1. Town and village re-building and re-enlivening. A general effort after health, joy, and beauty; a policy of weal in place of 'wealth', festivals, folk-schools, eisteddfods, stadiums.

2. The establishment of a dozen new universities of experimental types, recognizing crafts, art, and all kinds of research, production, making, and doing.

E

3. National old-age hospitals in place of the feared and hateful workhouse infirmaries.

4. Country redemption and general tidying up, burying old tins, burning old paper, and tearing down insulting advertisements.

5. Making the railway system rational, efficient, and orderly: our stations and station-yards must be nearly the worst in the world.

6. An Irish Channel tunnel and finely constructed railway to a port on the Atlantic. A really worthy gateway to the West, a British Appian Way.

7. The setting up of a Ministry for Civilization, which would recognize the need for national story, music, drama, and art, and give some attention to our wretched coins, stamps, public heraldry, and 'brilliant ceremonies'.

8. The re-building of the greater part of London.

9. The embanking and guiding our overflooding rivers, and planting the wasteful hedges with fruit-trees.

10. The organizing of summer camps attached to all large towns, where some of the experience gained during the war might be maintained.

Every county might experiment in building a new town. Every town might throw out a garden suburb. Every village might build at least one stout and neat little house which might be let to some one who has suffered. It would be perfectly easy to put a worthy commemorative inscription and list of names on such a building. Organized labour could make use of the memorial motive in founding a town for craft teaching and industrial research, also for experiments in well living in small houses. The ideal is certainly the house which could be worked without slavery and without the greasy waste and hidden squalor of rich houses. How best to live with the least consumption is an aim which might safely be put before all people when a time comes for considering possible ideals in civilization. Here indeed would be a fair field for the play of our competitive energies. We need a practice of economic experiment and research, health laboratories, group living, community hospitality, better cooking, and some human amusements which don't pay dividends. The material appliances of our civilization are altogether inadequate. We badly need Wisdom in her works as well as in her words. We have to think of civilization as a whole, as an ambition, as experiment. If we could establish a wisdom council on this one object of making worthy memorials the precedent might widen, and it might at least be remembered that even Government must recognize that it has to be more than an 'administration'. Some day when we have learnt not to slay ideals with our 'sense of humour' we may find it desirable to have a Minister for Civilization.

The ever-accelerating momentum of modern life—or existence—has passed into eccentric orbits, and we seem to prefer to patch wreckage rather than to make a plain way. A special effort is necessary to find the bare data for rational production. It is hardly possible to get it understood that a 'work of art' is not a design thrown off by a genius, but it is a piece of honest work consecrated to a noble purpose. At least a work of art implies workmanship. Labour of course must be cast into appropriate forms, but the craftsmen saw to that before 'design' became the tastes and whims of middlemen. We have to wake to the understanding that nobody really cares for 'art' sterilities, and we are not even able to do them speciously well. After the mayor's speech at the unveiling function we turn our backs on our monuments, and never speak of them again; except of some which we make into whetstones to sharpen our wits, or rather our tongues.

Those strange peoples the ancients made memorials simply and directly, building their hearts into them. We have heart, too, but not frankness; we seek manner, not speech; and we spend our strength in preliminary anxieties, so that the works themselves are born tired.

The very names we call the 'styles' confess all. Designs in Greek, Roman, Byzantine, Gothic, Elizabethan, and Georgian styles are only waxworks in a chamber of horrors.

Ornamental design is dealing with signs and symbols, the saying of something in another mode of language. Our hope in some abstract beauty which shall say nothing, being without natural affection, meaning, feeling, heart or head, is altogether vain. These designs in the 'grand manner' are pompous nullities, which only advertise that dulling of the spirit we call education. In seeking the beautiful nothing we seek a ghost which is not there. May we not sometime learn from our failures, and so make these, too, of worth? Must hope be always the bud of disappointment? A designer takes infinite pains to be quite safe and non-committal, and then committees sit on the 'design' till it has finally been made dull and dead. Nothing living can pass through the torture of anxious committees. In a work of art courage is needed and an untired mind in the worker. Every fine work is the embodied enthusiasm of maker-poets—we cannot take fire from the cold ashes of committee compromises or the reflected flames of stylists.

We are not ready to produce works of art consciously poetic—wherefore again let us do things obviously useful for life's sake. Above all things the returned soldiers, or their widows and mothers when they return no more, need houses. Would not a pleasant, tidy little house in every village bearing on a panel, MEMORIAL COTTAGE, and other words and names, be the most touching, significant, and beautiful of all possible monuments? The people asked for houses and we have given them stones.

Chapter VII

The Architecture of Adventure [1]

By adventure I mean what to me seems to have been the living force and active principle of all architecture, the spirit of experiment in building. It is somewhat curious that of all the thousands of books which exist on architecture there is hardly one known to me which deals with the subject without some qualifying adjective, as Greek, Roman, or Gothic; or which asks what is the greatest common denominator of all of them which might come near being architecture itself, past, present, and future. And here, at the risk of some repetition, I must say what I think we are compelled to mean by this ambiguous and abused word. I have often tried to speak of ordinary customary building as being one with architecture; architecture, in fact, is only building 'writ large'. But if, having two words, we desire to give them separate meanings, consistent though separate, then we must agree to mean by architecture building enhanced by sculpture and painting—that is, building 'completely furnished', as Morris says. Architecture would then stand to building as opera stands to music. Architecture must thus, according to our choice, either mean building in

[1] Royal Institute of British Architects, 1910.

general, or building intensified by accessory arts. In any case, mere needful and experimental building is the main substance, force, and origin of the art. When the higher architecture has appeared in the world, it has come as the result of spontaneous interaction of the arts; the architect has wrought according to custom, need, and demand, while sculptors, painters, and the rest have done the same. The resulting unity was not imposed by an architect's artistic ideal, but because all expressed their thought in a common current language.

Architecture or building, so far as at any given moment it deals with known traditional needs, should be customary; so far as it has to meet changing conditions and ideals it must be experimental. For the customary part practical craft education would be best; but how to meet changing needs, especially when one of the changes is the breakdown of custom itself, is a new and urgent question. However desirable it might be to continue in old ways or revert to past types, it is, I feel on reviewing the attempts which have been made, impossible. We have passed into a scientific age, and the old practical arts, produced instinctively, belong to an entirely different era.

I have long been interested in the search for sources of inspiration in our art, always with the immediate inquiry before me as to what may be an inspiration to the architects of to-day and to-morrow. I have come to the conclusion that any basis on which there can be some general agreement over a long space of time will produce architecture of a sort. The one thing essential is this agreement, so that a process of development may be set up by continuous experiment. A school of art is only generated by intensity, the heat of a common pressure. The only possible basis of agreement at the present time is the scientific method.

In a former Paper [1] I tried to examine the Greek theory that architecture was to be reached through a system of ratios. This idea could only be applied to a thing as fixed and simple in general type, as a temple. It belongs to a conception of holy architecture. The Greeks probably took over the notion of such a method from the Egyptians; in any case, it belongs to many ancient peoples: the Arabs, for instance, find consolation (so do I) in the fact that the temple of Mecca is supposed to be built so that its length, breadth, and height are equal. The Greek thought on the matter was very clear-cut and simple. It was no mere talk of the wonders of proportion, which ends by pointing out that in any work there is, as a matter of fact, relation between the parts. For instance, in any given picture, there *is* some relation between the red and the blue; but this relation is not fixed for all pictures, and it was not fixed for any particular one until it was finished. I want to be clear about this: that 'proportion' strictly means what it meant to the Greeks, a definite prearranged relation of measured quantities. This view is, perhaps, most clearly brought out in the case of sculpture, to which they naturally came to apply similar schemes of related measures. Polyclitus, the contemporary and equal of Pheidias, wrote a book on the subject, called *The Canon*, and made a celebrated statue to illustrate it. The head was one-seventh of the total height, and all the other parts had definite ratios. Moreover, a saying of his is preserved: 'Success in

[1] 'The Theory of Greek Architecture', *R.I.B.A. Journal*, 8 Feb. 1908.

art is attained by exactness in a multitude of arithmetical proportions.' Greek artists seem to have agreed to such a theory, and although it was ill founded, yet the myth led them on—that is, they set about discovering perfection; and we know what wonders they accomplished in consequence.

The Romans as certainly agreed in a desire for bigness and splendour, and they, too, succeeded according to their desires. The Arab builders fell into a love of bright colours, baked into shining tiles, and this, too, gave a character to *their* art. Any strong and general interest in building felt by a people will produce a living school of art. There is no one perfect school, there is an infinitude of conceivable perfections.

.   .   .   .

Engineers' Architecture. With all these variables, however, there has been one constant—the *building* interest; the delight in experimental structure, the adventure into the unknown.

I must fortify myself here with some historical data, in proof of what would otherwise be mere assertion. Notwithstanding the Greek theory of temple architecture, their architects, as a matter of fact, seem nearly always to have been engineers; and it is this engineering interest in architecture which I am about to trace. Their legendary craft-master was the mechanician Daedalus. Callicrates, the builder of the Parthenon, also built the great fortification called the Long Walls. Hippodamus, the celebrated architect, also of the age of Pericles, fortified the Piraeus, and was an expert in town planning.

Archimedes himself was counted among their seven great architects.

The engineering element in Roman architecture is most marked, and it was this, indeed, which entirely burst the old bottles of tradition, and transformed the art into one of daring structural adventure. Most of the great Roman architects seem to have been engineers in the strict sense. Even Vitruvius, who was so much of a reactionary, was official keeper of war-engines, and he tells us that architecture had three branches, building, dialling, and mechanics; meaning by the last the construction of military and other engines. Trajan's favourite architect followed the army and built his wonderful military bridge over the Danube. Architects in Rome were called 'machinatores', also 'structores', and 'magistri'. Architect was a more general term which included ordinary workmen.[1]

The identity between engineers and architects continued into the Byzantine period, and all the great architects of the time of Justinian seem to have been engineers. Anthemius, the architect of Sta Sophia, is called the 'mechanikos', and we are told that 'he was an inventor of machines and reached the summit of mathematical knowledge'. Indeed, he has left a book on the subject. Associated with him was, as Procopius says, 'another mechanic called Isidorus'. 'They were the most suitable of all mankind for the purpose.' Isidorus the Younger, who re-erected the dome after its fall, had been employed in building the fortified military outpost, Zenobia. The famous and beautiful Church of the Virgin at Jerusalem was built for Justinian by Theodorus, called architect

[1] Cabrol's *Dict.*, s.v. Architect.

and 'machinarius'.[1] The learned Benedictine, Leclercq, says that this name of mechanician, carrying the idea of constructor, is found in all epochs of the Lower Empire.

When we reach the Middle Ages we meet with evidence which shows the same state of things. Alnoth, the celebrated master of works of Henry II, was an engineer. In France, Eudes, the favourite master of Louis IX, went with him to Palestine and constructed the walls of Jaffa. The custom is well represented in the sketch-book of the architect Villard de Honnecourt, which treats of building, sculpture, geometry, and machines. Amongst his notes, which include an essay on Perpetual Motion, and many mechanical devices like power-saws, pile-drivers, cross-bows, and war-engines, is one on the construction of a floor out of timber too short to bear across the space. This I note because we shall meet with it again.

The great mediaeval buildings are, all the best critics unite in telling us, solutions of problems of how to throw stones high into the air, and balance them there. A great French castle or cathedral was not designed as beauty, it was developed along a line of experiment as surely as the great ocean liners have been so developed. We may almost regard it as an accident of traditional custom that the bishops and the people liked to have the fronts of their churches covered with didactic sculptures and their windows filled with stained glass. The essential construction, however, was conceived by any of the great masters as a

[1] Cler. Ganneau in Q. S. of Pal. Expl. Fund, 1898, p. 251. See also what Procopius says of Chryses of Alexandria: 'A clever engineer who served Justinian as an architect.'

problem of stress and poise, just as the designer of the Forth Bridge so conceived his problem.

.   .   .   .

The Renaissance. The scholars of the Renaissance set themselves systematically to learn all that might be learnt. This is the mark of the new birth of learning. Its spirit is most completely manifested in that extraordinary man Leonardo da Vinci, and our own Bacon fully grasped and expounded the theory. But in building art a strange thing happened—as Morris puts it, 'the past slew the present'; 'strange to say, to this living body of social and scientific New Birth was bound the corpse of a past art. On every other side it bade men look forward, on the side of art it bade them look back.' It is evident that one of the subjects opened up for scholarly investigation was the mighty architecture of Rome. Under other circumstances it might have been possible that the principles—the science of construction—should have been studied, and not the mere fashion of the outward adorning, but it was not to be. One reason why this was so may be suggested: Italian patriotism seized on the ideal of reviving the past architecture of Rome, and putting away the intermediate manner of building which had been brought in by the German conquerors.

The notebooks and studies of Leonardo, however, show that it was always phenomena and principles which interested *him*. Large sections of his manuscripts are devoted to abstract exercises in planning, to considerations of dome-building and other structural possibilities, as well as to studies in engineering, machine-making, fortification, and canals. Amongst his schemes is one for a town, for Leonardo was a pioneer in town planning as well as in aviation.

This scheme comprises a system of low-level streets for commercial purposes, and an upper residential stratum. The roads slope to the higher level outside the walls, and within they are connected by bridges, while the lower region is reached by staircases and large areas opened to it for light. 'Those', he says, 'who would go through the whole place by the high-level streets can do so, and he who would go below can do so. The stairs must be circular because the corners of square ones are always foul.' Another scheme is for combined streets and canals, by which cellars were made accessible to boats. 'Let the width of the street', he says, 'be equal to the average height of the houses.' An important section deals with domes, being, as Richter says, 'theoretical and ideal researches made in order to obtain a clear understanding of the laws which must govern the construction of a great central dome with smaller ones grouped around it. In these sketches [I am still quoting] Leonardo seems to have exhausted every imaginable combination to illustrate the consequences resulting from a given principle.' Quite so; he was the first, that is, to enter on a systematic inquiry as to the mechanics of architecture.

Among these studies into abstract architectural possibilities is an examination of the puzzle floor which I have already mentioned, it is caught up, investigated, and at once universalized into a principle—that of the Japanese lattice (see fig. 1).[1]

[1] Still later the puzzle floor was published by Serlio, and an example of it was made a wonder of at our Royal Society (see *Parentalia*).

FIG. I

FIG. 2

Another study which so far as I know has not been explained is the four-flight inter-winding staircase (see fig. 2), which afterwards appears in Palladio, and which Inigo Jones thought the Italian architect must have taken from Chambord, where it had been realized. Now, as Chambord was begun just at the time when Leonardo was living at Blois, and as the section of his studies which contains this remarkable exercise relates to the design for a palace for Francis I, one may, I think, conclude that this stair was Leonardo's invention. All these studies were probably for the complete treatise on architecture which he contemplated producing.[1] The spirit in which he followed investigation is expressed in an outburst so high-pitched that I am almost ashamed to quote it: 'O marvellous Necessity, thou with supreme wisdom constrainest all effects to be the direct result of their causes, and by irrevocable law every natural action obeys thee by the shortest possible process. O wonderful stupendous Necessity, the theme and artifice of Nature, the Eternal law.' In another place he says: 'There is no certainty where one may not apply any of the mathematical sciences.'

The only other artist of the Renaissance known to me who caught the idea of investigation principles—the scientific spirit—was Dürer, and he possibly had access to Da Vinci's notebooks. In his manuscripts in the British Museum are some studies for domes of a parabolic

[1] Richter.

section, and some exercises in plan schemes. The dome of parabolic section was 'in the air' long before Wren in turn seized on it.

Wren's Teaching. For England and more modern times we fortunately have some records of the thoughts of Wren on the art he practised. Although Wren was not a world-genius like Leonardo da Vinci, he was in many respects an English Leonardo, and the one architect we have had whose formal thought matters. I say formal as opposed to the flashes of insight of a dozen men like Pugin. Wren's was a great intellect most highly trained in all the science and philosophy of an ample age. He had been marvellously precocious, and during a very long life tried to satisfy an infinite curiosity by patient investigation. More even than a great artist, Wren was a great man. It may be somewhat curious to note here how often admirable practical skill in the arts may be linked to great poverty of thought in theoretic exposition, so that the splendid achievement of a Palladio or a Chambers in active work may be accompanied by mere twaddle of explanation and rhetoric.

Some recent writers have rather lightly taken it for granted that there must be some mistake as to Wren's scientific attainments, but we have the consensus of opinion of his contemporaries and of modern mathematical and astronomical experts that he was a powerful original genius. He is said to have been the first to make a model of the moon's surface as seen through a telescope, and the first to draw minute objects through a microscope. He and his friend, Robert Hook, another scientific architect, were conversant with the general law of

gravitation before Newton brought it to a proof. Newton, in a letter to Halley, speaks of a visit he paid to Sir
Christopher, in which they 'discussed the problem of
determining the heavenly motions on philosophic principles. You are acquainted with Sir Christopher; pray
know when and where he first learnt the decrease of the
force in the duplicate ratio of the distance from the
centre.' Halley replied that 'Sir Christopher told him that
Mr. Hook had frequently told him that he had proved it,
but that he never was satisfied that his demonstration was
correct.' That is, the problem of gravity had been discussed by Wren and Hook and its actual law stated before
Newton proved it in a convincing way.[1]

This same Hook says of him, 'Since the time of Archimedes there scarce ever met in one man in so great perfection, such a mechanical hand and so philosophical a
mind'; Hook again, in his treatise on comets, gives a
method of determining their parallax 'invented by that
incomparable mathematician, Dr. Christopher Wren'.
These things are beyond my knowledge, but I know that
they represent wonderful powers.

It was after one of Wren's professional lectures on
astronomy that, in 1660, a committee was formed which
instituted the Royal Society, then described as 'a Philosophical Society for the Promotion of Physico-Mathe-
matical Experiment'. Wren was instructed to sum up its
scheme, and in this he explained that it was to 'make
provision *for Natural experimental philosophy*'.

Wren was almost certainly the first in England to apply

[1] *Dictionary of National Biography*, under 'Newton'. See also Museum
of Royal Society in Hatton's *New View of London*, 1708.

the methods of scientific investigation to the laws of structure, and Hook is said to have been the first who stated the mechanical properties of the arch. In Wren's earliest report on St. Paul's he says that it might be affirmed of its vault: 'Not by an architect taking his measures from the Ancients, but by a Geometrician—this part being liable to demonstration—that the roof was ever too heavy for its butment.'

We are fortunate in possessing records, however slight, of Wren's systematic thought on architecture in some fragments which have been printed in *Parentalia*, and by Miss Phillimore. The teachings of such a man on his chosen art should have great value and weight, but they have been strangely overlooked and have never, so far as I know, been commented on. It seems clear from these fragments that he contemplated writing a history of architecture and also a general philosophy of its first principles, both possibly to be combined in one work. The fragments belong to a time late in his long life, for Wren speaks of the vaults of St. Paul's as in being. The notes may have been written when, over eighty, he had retired from active work to pass his time in contemplation and studies. Miss Phillimore has printed what seems to be an introduction to the historical study of classical buildings published in *Parentalia*. This introductory part was cut away, possibly because it dealt with subjects like the Ark of Noah and the Temple of Solomon, but there are some interesting general remarks by way of introduction. The part given in *Parentalia* contains a critical examination of Pliny's accounts of the Temple of Diana at Ephesus, and of the Mausoleum, also a description of

F

the 'Temple of Mars Ultor' and the 'Temple of Peace' in Rome. In the preliminary remarks which I shall quote it appears that his intention in the proposed work was to give 'a larger idea of the whole art' of architecture, and he thus began:

'Whatever a man's sentiments are upon mature deliberation, it will still be necessary for him in a conspicuous work to preserve his undertaking from censure, and *to accommodate his designs to the gust of the age he lives in, though it appears to him less rational.* I have found no little difficulty to bring persons otherwise of good genius to think anything in architecture would be better than what they have heard commended. Many Gothic forms of cathedrals are to be seen in our country and many had been seen abroad, which they liked the better for being not much different from ones in England. This humour with many is not yet eradicated and, therefore, I judge it not improper to endeavour to reform the generality to a better taste in architecture by giving *a larger idea of the whole art, beginning with the reasons and progress of it* from the most remote antiquity, touching chiefly on some things which have not been remarked by others. *The project of building is as natural to mankind as to the birds.*'

In the fragment printed in *Parentalia* we have an admirable statement of the utility of architecture in the State in a phrase which might be taken as a motto by town-planning associations: '*Architecture has its political use; public buildings being the ornament of a country; it establishes a Nation, draws people and commerce; makes the people love their native country, which passion is the great original of all great actions in a Commonwealth.*'

Rather extravagant that may seem to us, but a practical proof follows out of history. 'The emulation of the cities of Greece was the true cause of their greatness. The obstinate valour of the Jews, occasioned by the love of their Temple, was a cement that held together that people for many ages, through infinite changes. The care of public decency and convenience was a great cause of the establishment of the Low Countries and of many cities in the world. Modern Rome subsists still by the ruins and imitation of the old.'

'Architecture aims at Eternity; and therefore *is the only thing incapable of modes and fashions in its principles*.' 'The Orders are not only Roman and Greek, but Phoenician, Hebrew, and Assyrian, *being founded upon the experience of all ages*, promoted by the vast treasures of the great monarchs and skill of the greatest artists and geometricians, *every one emulating each other*.' The Orders, that is, were admirable so far as they embodied much experiment and long experience. And then he proceeds, in more general language: 'Beauty, firmness and convenience are the principles: the two first depend upon geometrical reasons of optics and statics; the third only makes the variety.' The geometrical, that is structural, principles are eternal, but a changing element is brought in by new needs and new ideas of convenience. 'There are two causes of beauty—natural and customary. Natural is from geometry, consisting in uniformity, that is quality, and proportion. Customary beauty is begotten by the use, as familiarity breeds a love to things not in themselves lovely. Here lies the great occasion of errors, but always the true *test is natural or geometrical beauty*. Geometrical figures are naturally more beautiful than irregular ones: the square, the circle are most beautiful; next the parallelogram and the oval. There are only two beautiful positions of straight lines, perpendicular and horizontal; *this is from Nature and consequently necessity*, no other than upright being firm.' He then passes to the expression of some very interesting particular views based largely on his favourite Roman architecture; but enough has been said to show that he accepted that only as embodying a vast stock of past experience, and he knew that the real basis of architecture was necessity, law, geometry. Further on he says so still more clearly in the opening of the second tract (or second chapter of a general treatise) which begins thus:

'Modern authors who have treated of architecture seem generally to have little more in view, but to set down the proportions of columns, &c., as they are distinguished into Doric, Ionic, Corinthian, and Composite, finding them in the ancient fabrics. *Though more arbitrarily used than they care to acknowledge*, they have reduced them to rules, though in their own nature *they are but the modes and fashions of those ages wherein they were used*. Although architecture contains many excellent parts besides the ranging of pillars, yet curiosity may lead us to consider whence this affection arose originally, so as to judge nothing beautiful but what was adorned with columns, even where there was no real use for them. It will be to the purpose to examine whence proceeded this affectation of a mode which hath continued now at least 3,000 years, and the rather because it may *lead us to the grounds of architecture* and by what steps this humour of colonnades came into practice.' He thinks the habit of mind first was

rooted when men sacrificed in groves. Then he passes on
to what was evidently to be the chief content of his work,
the consideration of the true grounds of architecture in
structural law, in these words: '*It seems very unaccountable
that the generality of our late architects dwell so much upon this
ornamental, and so slightly pass over the geometrical, which is
the most essential part of architecture.* For instance, can an
arch stand without butment sufficient? If the butment be
more than enough it is an idle expense of materials; if too
little it will fall; and so for any vaulting, and yet no
author hath given a true and universal rule for this nor
hath considered all the various forms of arches.' Wren
then proceeds to investigate the laws of stability by consideration of the centres of gravity of the several parts,
basing himself on 'Archimedes and the modern geometricians who have treated of centres of gravity'. [1] His
first demonstration regarding the arch is so simple and
illustrates his method so well that I give its essence in
general words. If the model of *half an arch* with its abut-
ment (a diagram of an arch in a square of wall is given)
will stand of itself, then the two halves when brought
together into a complete arch will stand. 'So it appears',
he says, 'that the design where there are arches must be
regulated by the art of statics and the duly *poising of all
parts to equiponderate. Hence I conclude that all designs must in
the first place be brought to this test or be rejected.* I have
examined some celebrated works, as the Pantheon, and
judge there is more butment than necessary. I suppose the
architect provided against earthquakes. The different

---

[1] He would have been delighted in the recently discovered and just
published treatise on the Centre of Gravity by Archimedes.

forms of vaulting [he goes on] are necessary to be considered, both as they were used by the ancients and the moderns [i.e. mediaeval builders], whether Freemasons or Saracens.' He then reviews different types of vaulting—Roman, Mediaeval, and Byzantine—and gives us the interesting information that he adopted the form of vaults used at St. Paul's from Sta Sophia, 'because it was the lightest manner and requires less butment; I have therefore preferred it to any other way used by architects'.

The theory of architecture here erected on wide foundations of knowledge, historical and experimental, is truly a general explanation, a philosophy of architecture, and we shall far rather be disciples of Wren by understanding his mind than by vainly copying the forms of things which he himself used more or less under protest (as in the case of the balustrade) in different relations, and, as he himself says, according to 'the gust' of the age in which he lived. I may say here that no adequate account of Wren himself and his accomplishment exists except the remarkable life contributed to the *Dictionary of National Biography* by the man of the last generation who was best qualified to understand him, and I wish that it could be printed together with Wren's own teachings, on which I have here ventured to comment. It would, I think, make the best foundation book for all our proposed teaching, for it should stir ambition, clear thought, and do much to shake off the dull artistic inertia and contented utterance of theoretic platitude which too much besets us all.

Wren tells us that he designed the beautiful saucer domes of St. Paul's by borrowing them from Sta Sophia because they were the most mechanically perfect that he could find. Some sketches for the great dome (see fig.) show that its section was conceived as conforming to a general parabolic curve rising from the plinths of the great piers and passing through the abutments and over the crown of the so-called cone. I say 'so-called', because, with its rounded top, its section is a parabola. Wren saw, and probably was the first of architects to do so, that 'necessity', which he equates with 'nature', must be one

with beauty. We are told that he always preferred his earlier scheme for St. Paul's, and it is plain he must have done so, for that has unity; the whole was a domical structure, not a structure with a dome. Some residuum of the idea is found in the present plan, for the nave proper is made equal to the choir and a vestibule bay is added in front. There is under the strictest limitations of law wide room for choice, of course. For in-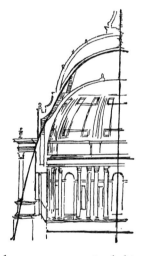stance, Wren doubtless might have counterpoised his main vaults by another means than the high screen on the aisles; but the expedient is perfectly scientific, and probably he borrowed the idea from mediaeval buildings, looking on it as a continuous pinnacle.

.   .   .   .

Conclusions. I have tried to show in the foregoing extracts and comments that the living central stem of architecture has always been rooted in the spirit of active experiment and adventure for the further satisfaction of needs and desires. Two views as to the meaning and content of architecture have been held, and perhaps still are—at least some people seem to think they hold them. (1) That there is a *thing*, Architecture—perhaps revealed in the one perfect form of classical art, or manifested more or less in different forms in divers times, as Greek and Gothic architecture. Further, it is to be attained by a special sense in the artist. (2) That the essence of architecture is proportion, the discovery and use of definite ratios, and that by this method of proportioning an absolute architecture may be embodied. There is a third view which holds that architecture is primarily building according to the natural laws of structure and stability, according to need and order, and always with care and finish; that it must ever vary with ever-changing conditions, and that this ordinary building may have associated with it painted stories and sculptured stories, or inlays and fretted works and gildings, while the essential architecture is still structure, and the method of architectural growth is by continuous experiment in the possibilities of structure. I must safeguard myself from being thought to urge any quest of originality. Quite the reverse. I am satisfied that all search for it just blocks the way, with our preconceptions and limitations, to any possibility of realizing a true originality, which properly is of the root, not of the appearance. True originality is to be found by those who, standing on the limits of the sphere of the known, reach out naturally to some apprehension and understanding of what is beyond; it is the next step in an orderly development.

What I *do* urge, in the simplest and plainest words, is concentration on practical, experimental, and scientific education. What we most need at the present time is the accumulation of power; we want high mechanical training, wide practical experience, and great geometry. And then we want to cover the field by a systematic research into possibilities. The possibilities of walls and vaults, and of the relations between the walls and the cell, and between one cell and another, want investigating, as Lord Kelvin investigated the geometry of crystalline structures and the 'packing of cells'. In my view, it is true, such a training would not include the whole of architecture, but it would, I believe, open the way to the best we can attain. We might hope thus to give up hugging the coasts of the known, to sail boldly forth under the stars. Thus, and thus only for us, may we enter again upon the Architecture of Adventure.

In a late number of the *R.I.B.A. Journal* is a paper which touches on the imaginative and poetic side of architecture, and, in the main, seems true enough, but it hardly sufficiently, to my mind, recognizes the actual facts of to-day. For instance, it says: 'There is a phrase, "reason in building," which is the favourite catchword of the moment with a certain class of persons fond of oracular utterances.' It then proceeds to say that it is 'imaginative reason' which is wanted. Why, yes, of course. When we can get it I should like it very much; and I do find it in the Forth Bridge; I saw it last spring in a concrete railway viaduct, and in the autumn in the smart tidiness of the city of Munich, in the ironwork of the little wayside stations high up in the Chamounix Valley; in the new barracks at Strasburg, and a new railway water-tower at Metz. I saw it the other day in a photograph of the last great sailing-ship built, a five-master, I think, and bearing a vast area of swelling canvas. Some brick-kilns have the beauty of Byzantine churches, and the most romantic modern buildings I know are the oast-houses of Kent. All these are, indeed, works of imaginative reason, and one may look at them with startled interest. In the same number with the objection to mere reason a quotation is made from a speech by Mr. James Bryce, who at least is an expert on European history. He remarks that the historian of architecture when he comes to the nineteenth century is at a loss, and goes on to ask, 'Now, is not the time about due when you must be beginning to do something desperate?'

Building has been, and may be, an art, imaginative, poetic, even mystic and magic. When poetry and magic are in the people and in the age they will appear in their arts, and I want them, but there is not the least good in saying, 'Let us go to and build magic buildings. Let us be poetic.' Yet let me say again, it is because I want these things that I face this problem.

If I may be a 'self-constituted' educational adviser to the Institute of Architects, and express such a personal view, I, too, would say, 'It is about time to do something desperate'. We should devote the whole of the next session to papers on constructive science, get Professor Karl Pearson to give us the result of his researches on the arch, Professor Perry to draw up a report on the application of mathematical inquiry to structures, and Mr. Dunn should lecture us on ordinary modern constructive problems. As talking of reason in design is to be tabooed as a self-evident truism, some one who is prepared to commit suicide should examine the prevalence of *irrationality* in modern buildings. The scientific side of our examinations should be rapidly screwed up, and the archaeological side as rapidly unscrewed. All our travelling studentships should be made to bear on the same quarter. Pugin students should be made to analyse varieties of mediaeval vaults, and Soane students varieties of staircase arrangement. Tites should be sent to study French railway stations, Grissells to work at German hotels, and Godwins to American hospitals.

I am anxious to repeat that I have not proposed to speak of the whole of architecture: the sublime sculptures of the Parthenon, the glittering mosaics of the vaults of St. Mark's, the solemn splendour of the glass of Chartres, and all the fear, mystery, rapture, delight and play which have been wrought into them; their energy, their pride, and their loveliness; and all their wreathings, frettings, veneerings, and inlays. Although I have not spoken of these, again I say it is because I want just such as these—but different —that I have spoken at all. I want pathetic beauty in the cottage and in the barn, the most exquisite order, freshness, and efficiency in our town streets, the uttermost of costly majesty in the city's public palace, and still something beyond for our cathedrals, some expression of infinite aspiration. It is because I want all these, if it may be, or even less if it will be, that I have set myself to consider how they might be attained, and it is my own conclusions on the matter that I have now put before you. We need first the natural, the obvious, and, if it will not offend to say so, the reasonable, so that to these which might seem to be under our own control, may be added we know not how or what of gifts and graces. Thus may we hope to combine the two realities, the reality of natural necessity and common experience with the reality of the philosophers, which is the ideal, and to reconcile again Science with Art.

.   .   .   .

Of course, I have written this paper from a special area that I marked down, and I hope that I have been careful to limit myself by saying that I did not think—again and again I tried to say it—that it exhausted the whole of the possibilities of architecture. My main thought, however, was this. The method of design to a modern mind can only be understood in the scientific, or in the engineer's sense, as a definite analysis of possibilities—not as a vague poetic dealing with poetic matters, with derivative ideas of what looks domestic, or looks farmlike, or looks ecclesiastical—the dealing with a multitude of flavours—that is what architects have been doing in the last hundred years. They have been trying to deal with a set of flavours—things that looked like things but that were not the things themselves. Old farm-houses and cottages are things themselves—cottages and farm-houses. Now we, the best of us, are trying to build things which shall *look like* farmhouses and look like cottages, and so on. It suggests to me a story that my friend Mr. Horsley told me twenty-five years ago. Passing down a back street in London he saw a card in a window, 'Fine jam, good strawberry flavour, 4*d*. a lb.' It is not the strawberry flavour we want in building, it is good sound food.

Once more I venture to say that the living stem of building-design can only be found by following the scientific method.

Chapter VIII

Modern German Architecture and what we may learn from it [1]

IACCEPTED the invitation of the committee to lecture on this subject too readily, although, as a matter of fact, I did so with great hesitation. The times are too tremendous for talk, and in serious times the expression of any views which are narrowly personal is a mere impertinence. In some, in many, respects we must be the most capable and gifted nation on the earth, and there is a form of patriotism which would rest content in pride of these things. There is, however, also an intenser patriotic pride which hates to fall short in any worthy power or skill, and which would add to what we certainly have all of value in which we fail. There is a patriotism which would have London even as Athens and Florence, and cannot rest until we 'have built Jerusalem in England's green and pleasant land'. There might be a patriotism so proud that it would disdain to assert its virtues and be content with the acclamations and reverence of other peoples.

My right to speak of German architecture and arts and crafts comes from my having visited the country about

[1] Architectural Association, 1915.

half a dozen times, and having seen many of the most important cities, including Berlin. It was many years ago that I came to the personal conclusion that Germany was racing; that she had consciously divided up human activities and knowledge into departments, and had definitely set herself to outrun all other competitors in all of them. The guardians and directors of the State had, it seemed to me, substituted for the old customary methods and detached competitions in arts and sciences a clear and definite purpose of beating down all rivals and surpassing all emulation. This is not far-fetched; it has simply been the result of bringing in the Prussian war spirit into every phase of life. German science, of which I can only speak concerning archaeology, German industry, German architecture, have all been recast under the dominating desire to attack and to conquer. Think what this means if it is true—and something like it must be true—that at some time, forty or fifty years ago, the real leaders of the Prussian Power should have gathered together in some room and have decided to enter on such a definite campaign. German museums, German books, German machine industry and factories, the German theatre, and all the rest were to outclass the spontaneous productions of neighbour States. This being the end in view, all the necessary means were easy to see and to apply. The efforts of other peoples were studied, reported on, absorbed and their mistakes in many cases rectified. For it has been an essential part of the position that Germany, coming into the field as an attacking party, was able to select and experiment in a way that was impossible for those who, in many cases, had been the pioneers. This conquering spirit certainly carries far; we do not know how far, but it must have its limitations—it will, I think, dry up the sources of originality. It seems to me, although there is a certain absurdity in uttering individual opinions on the psychology of a colossal Empire, that the Prussian spirit runs to extremes; even organization may perhaps be over-organized, specialization be too specialized, and thoroughness be too thorough. Germany perhaps tends to the unmeasured. Domesticity and feeding seem to an outsider to be done without measure—education and erudition are perhaps carried beyond due measure, and violence is certainly made violent beyond measure. They seem to have amended the Greek doctrine of the mean into 'everything beyond measure'. In casting about for reasons for this I have sometimes thought that one might be found in the fact that Northern Germany was never brought within the circle of ancient civilization.

The most striking general characteristics of Germany to my mind are those of great size of the number of cities which are obviously architectural and centres of learning and of the dignity of the public services like the railways and trams. The size we cannot, of course, emulate, and we hardly perhaps realize the immensity of what by recent developments has practically become one Germany from the North Sea to the Adriatic, with a population nearly three times as large as ours. But the dignity of the cities and of the services must be acknowledged and praised.

I began by making notes of many points to speak on, but I shall limit myself to two.

The first thing in the arts which we should learn from Germany is how to appreciate English originality. Up to about twenty years ago there had been a very remarkable development of English art in all kinds. For five or six years, round about the year 1900, the German Government had attached to its Embassy in London an expert architect, Herr Muthesius, who became the historian (in German) of the English free architecture. All the architects who at that time did any building were investigated, sorted, tabulated, and, I must say, understood. Then, just as our English free building arrived, or at least 'very very nearly did', there came a timid reaction and the re-emergence of the catalogued 'styles'. It is equally true or even more true that the German advances in industrial design have been founded on the English arts and crafts. They saw the essence of our best essays in furniture, glass, textiles, printing, and all the rest, and, laying hold on them, coined them into money, while our Press, caught up into an eddy of devilish bright writing, set about to kill the whole thing. Just as we gave Germany many of the industrial ideas which she has so thoroughly exploited—the extracting of aniline dyes, for example; just as she took up the arts and crafts experiments which we employed critics to destroy at home; so we first seem to have arrived at the thought of an architecture which should develop in its own sphere, and not be for ever casting back to disguise itself in the skins which it had long ago sloughed off—or, like the dog of Scripture, eat its dinner twice over. (Even this image, however, is inadequate; the ideal seems to be that the architectural dog should for ever and ever re-swallow the same meal.) German architects have seized on this theory of a 'real architecture'—or they have reached it for themselves. Meanwhile we have been caught up in

G

one of our recurring reactions. Architecture is not seen as one of the forms in which the national energy, intellect, and spirit shall expand, but it is diverted and maimed and caged into formulas which are not only dead, but never had life.

The second thing which I wish we would earnestly compete in is PUBLIC WORKS. There are great things in a nation's life which cannot be estimated, and it is quite possible that for a dozen or fifteen years we have been living in the shadow of this terrible war and could do no other than we have done. But in our thought and in our effort as soon as may be we must set about public works everywhere and of every kind.

I take two instances from the newspapers of this month. We have had our recurring Thames Valley flood, which we get with surprise every eight or ten years. One morning my paper said that the fourteenth-century embankment of Chertsey was being watched with anxiety, and it was likely it would give way. Only a few years ago I went to Eton to see the discomfort of the school in another such flood. To any one who travels it is a marvel how streams are guided and controlled and bridged—and we only need the 'Happy Thought' that this may be, and shall be, the last Thames flood.

Now I give you a cutting from a recent paper: 'Describing a visit paid by him five years ago to the Berlin Military Technical Academy, Sir George Greenhill said it was a magnificent institution, such as our rulers assured us we could not afford. The whole place, with its laboratories and other opportunities for the pursuit of peaceful science, was kept as smart and noble as one of our old colleges.

There were plenty of outdoor artillery ranges close at hand for instructive work. Sixty officers were under instruction there for a course of three years, and their zeal was admirable. It was considered bad form not to give the best in return for the honour and glory of the Fatherland. It was a mournful contrast to revert to Woolwich, shabby and undisciplined, with the choice of a cellar under some stables or a kitchen and scullery and bare walls in a deserted hospital—there to organize victory at no expense. . . . We must put our trust in the junior ranks to push old Apathy from his stool and carry us through this war. . . . Our military science was under the rule of Thumb—the official genius whose fumbling method was considered a match for Disciplined Theory. "Thumb" was hostile to "Theory". He scented a dangerous rival.'

We must have magnificent institutions. There is not the least reason why we should not. They are paid for by taking money out of one pocket and putting it into the other, and the buildings then add to capital and plant. Expenditure of this sort is the only reasonable economy.

One thing the Germans have done is to organize a branch of orthodox and scientific political economy to deal with art and industries and the Arts and Crafts movement. We must press the London School of Economics to consider this question and all the questions which have to do with quality in production. I have often asked, and am never answered, what are the conditions of public expenditure on fine streets and noble buildings in a city? How far is it desirable to have clean and organized cities, how far shabby and miserable ones?

I would here like to appeal to our architectural papers

to consider for a time public works—not merely to chronicle them, but to ask for them, preach for them, and get them. The academic improvers of London are too apt to want to begin improving by pulling down some of the finest things we have, like the terrace in front of the National Gallery, or the Nelson Column. Our students are brought up to vain idealistic schemes of out-Haussmannizing Haussmann. We have no steady stream of opinion turned on everyday minor improvements, like the necessary putting in order of the underground stations which I travel by. The conception of public art would be such a welcome change to pictures of 'Mr. A.'s' Golf-cottage or 'Mr. X.'s' Billiard-room. Our great and noble architecture must be saved from being an adjunct of new-richness and week-ending.

A tremendous work has to be accomplished in England in improving all our villages and towns and the public services. Get into the habit of seeing things as they are, with the dirt, strewn paper, and orange-peel thrown in; don't acquiesce, don't be content. It is our business to improve the organization of public life as it is the doctor's to see to the public health. Go about saying that Charing Cross Station must be put out of the way, and all the other stations improved; advertisements must be kept in order, and the streets made clean. In your own work I would urge you to confidence and to go ahead. Throw away the hesitating carping spirit, venture on liking things; reserve criticism in the main for critics, and back up all active efforts. As much as lieth in you work with other men and other groups. Such association is an enormous gain of power. I see in our isolation the root of much of our artistic trouble. We are too apt to feel of another man, 'Oh, he's the fool that thinks I am a fool'.

Now at the end I must try to make a confusing distinction. I have found that when modern German effort in city-building is praised, people ask me, 'But do you like it?' It is a difficult question. Remember how little we really like before asking me if I like the hardness, glare, and brutality of modern Hanover, Strasburg, Magdeburg, or Cologne. They were not built for me to like, they were built for themselves. Besides, do I like modern Paris or London? Well, I don't. I do, however, greatly admire the wonderful efficiency and ambition of the Germans in city organization.

Chapter IX

Architecture and Modern Life [1]

To show that I have not been suddenly disturbed by the war, but that I was disturbed long before, I am venturing to quote a scrap from a paper I read to the Architectural Association about four years ago. 'Perhaps I should first try to justify my title ("Things to be done in Architecture") by giving reasons why anything should be done, but if anybody is satisfied with our towns as they are it would be hard to move them. I see, however, that all the countries of Europe and America are racing for the lead in civilization. Along with commercial strife there is a culture war going forward. This idea has perhaps only been consciously worked out in Germany, but it is obvious that there a consistent endeavour has been made during the last thirty or forty years to attain to a coherent type of modern city life. All has been done with forethought and system. Everywhere there is city pride and corporate life. Every city seems to have a large piece of pure country suburb where it goes out to picnic.'

It is this same question of the culture war, city pride, civilization which I want to bring before Architects, be-

[1] Royal Institute of British Architects, 1917.

cause I think it is their special cause. I may not succeed in putting my thought and meaning into words, but I want to beg of you to consider my *meaning* so far as I can get it expressed, and not to set about tearing my words to pieces. It has become a delightful amusement to us to differ in words, and in doing so we often ignore *things*. We really all agree in very much, but we are so eager for word arguments that if our very own opinions are uttered by some one else we are tempted to contradict them, or we raise confusing other questions in philosophy or politics; questions about freedom or tariff reform or education, or the leasehold system or the theory of aesthetics; but all the time we must agree that our institutions and thoughts being what they are we must, as architects, at least aim at order in our cities and towns. We cannot solve all the bordering questions, but being as we are we do as architects desire to improve the form and means of our civilization.

We think in words, and we talk of architecture and fine designs and art and style and so on, but we do not seem to notice with our eyes how little of these things we get in the real streets of the real towns we know—London and Leeds, Manchester and Macclesfield, Birmingham and Bristol. It is the real towns as they are that I want to get people to see, really to *see* with their eyes, not as statistics or as history, or as town planning on paper, as theory or style, but with their eyes, as they are: the approach, the railway station, the High Street, the food obtainable, the music, the general means of life and civilization, the houses, the shops, the public buildings, even the lamp-posts, and the ugly blotches of the advertisement disease.

If we agree in thinking that we should at least aim at bettering all these things, I want to suggest that we need a bigger centre and substance to work from than the personal one; we need a sense of citizenship, of public order, of national spirit. We need these for ourselves, and the Institute of Architects needs a collective outlook and purpose. It should be more than a large group of people of one calling; it needs to become the faculty for that part of civilization which is concerned with planning and building. The organized profession of Medicine is more than a trade union of doctors, it is the faculty for public health; Law is more than lawyers; so also I would have the Institute of Architects consider much more fully than it has done the whole question of modern building in civilization. If bodies of architects could walk down the Strand and along Holborn and see what all the architectural fuss during the last sixty years has produced they might wake up to the feeling that something must be done from the public point of view. It is not a matter of the whims, the ability, or the genius of the architect, it is a matter of civilization. A public conception of architecture would, I am sure, if it could be got into our minds be a steadying influence in design; but, more than this, the Institute should be a centre where a body of agreed opinion on city buildings could be brought together. I am clear in the distinction between city buildings and country buildings; the latter, as things are now, are much more personal, but in a city public propriety must be considered. No architect has any more right to put up an insulting building than to stand on the pavement and 'make faces' at us. We have to struggle continually to keep things even up to their present mark. Thus the West Central squares —such pleasant places forty years ago—have been allowed to run down and to be invaded by the most blatant vulgarity. So also our few circuses, such as those of Ludgate and Piccadilly, are disgraceful; that at the junction of Tottenham Court Road and Oxford Street is simply infamous. Our great railway stations must be the worst in the world, the new Tube stations are draughty and untidy —gashes in the street's side—and now they are running down into accepted dirt and ineptitude. All the streets are netted over and across and zigzag with sagging telegraph and telephone wires hitched on to weak parapets and trigged up to tottering chimneys—a shuddering sight when you take to notice these things. Fortunately most of us give up taking notice in infancy, and we go about communing with our own thoughts on the grandeur of architecture. No one except a wondering foreigner seems ever to have seen horrible Holborn and the silly Strand. We must attain to a sense of reality and see our cities as they actually are, and we must understand that architecture is concerned with buildings in the open air, often in the fog. The other day I went along a street which was bursting with a frenzy of design, but all the fronts had the usual frowning, smoke-grimed holes for windows, until I came to one which suddenly smiled. It had extra noise-preventing casements flush with the wall, and in a raking view one saw the glitter of sky reflections. It reopened a question as to a way of doing things which in my day had been a fad of style, but I saw that it must have been invented by Wren, or one of the building masters who saw things with their eyes. That is, when it was first done it was not called 'Queen Anne', but it was thought to be reasonable and pleasant.

Let me ask you to think in bigger units than we have done, think in cities and in civilizations, not in the little kinks of art-houses for stockbrokers' wives, with their garden 'pergolas' and 'smoking dens' all properly illustrated in the Press. Don't think of nice drawings or style-names and art talk, but in facts of life and building. For too long the noble art of building has been a sycophant to snobberies which do not lead to the strength of a nation. The art of building is one of the great things in the State and the body of architects properly make the faculty which has this in charge. I may unduly magnify my calling but I know nothing greater than the honest old craft of building.

Our public life has been shamefully let down in the appliances of civilization. Since the coming in of the railway flood we have just scraped along as if we felt that there was no abiding city. We have, as it were, stopped a hole with rags and tied up a break with string. Think of the post offices in the back-ends of grocers' shops; the police courts of unutterable squalor; the churches with their tawdries gas-lit in June; the leaky private houses with their cracked ceilings, and fireplaces making fog rather than heat. These things are not matters of taste and the aesthetic, they are matters of national strength, efficiency, and pride. Architecture deals with civilization, with the means of life, with towns, and we have to find a way to a richer life; we must have more of the 'plant' necessary for living in cities. Even in the excellent town-planning movement I have a fear that it may harden into a 'subject' called 'town planning' rather than be an out-burst of town vitality. Our towns have to be aroused; they must provide themselves with proud public buildings in well-ordered streets; they need better organized gymnastics with stadiums free of mud; they need better means of getting food, especially in the open air. It is not the climate that has prevented the existence of cafés in England—it may have been the brewing interest. We must preserve spaces of clean country near every town; we must have better national music; we must have a sense of something going on, and get out of the ring of stifling stagnation; we must set up something of the Greek idea of town worship, a sense of community interest and national spirit. A mere point of view; would that modify in any way our practice?—Besides, everybody recognizes the need for order, fitness, and soundness. Do they, indeed? Look at our streets as they are; look at the titles of the papers read during the last ten years at the Institute; read a year's leading articles in the architectural Press. I really think that looking on architecture as *Primarily the Art of Building Cities* might modify our practice, and if a sufficient body of people could be got to care I am sure it would. It might get into our teaching, into scholarship studies and essays, and at last it might work out into the streets. Now at once it might be seen as a reasonable basis for criticism; we should cease to be agitated about the drawings, the design, the style, but we should be solicitous about the building. Is it city-like, tidy, economical, well lighted, neighbourly, dignified, and so on? Is *this* good architecture? few of us would agree. Is *this* a good building? we should nearly all agree. We judge 'designs' for ideal sites and climates in summer weather, but the architects we know don't practise in heaven, but in places like London and Sheffield, where buildings have to live through long dark autumns, winters, and springs. We have to judge in the streets on January days, and all my lifetime there has been no judgement in the streets. I would have the 'art' words, like 'proportion', dropped because nobody knows what they mean, and I would have buildings tested by such generally understandable ideas as fitness, soundness, economy, efficiency, reasonableness, intelligibility, carefulness, science, mastery, seriousness, pleasantness, urbanity, vitality, boldness, humanity, adequateness, finish, discipline, frankness, directness, durability, clearness, order, homogeneity. There are two dozen words of the type which I should like to become the stock-in-trade of architectural critics; but it almost amuses me to think beforehand what good fun might be made of this in next week's papers. Sometimes I have a fear that we may die of our sense of humour. Outsiders and amateurs are ready to understand and sympathize if we can give them anything understandable, and I am often surprised by the fresh insight of University Extension students who have not been fully broken in to bugaboo architecture. We have had warnings for the last fifty years that style designing was of vital interest to nobody, and that it was one of the elements of unreality which were putting us to sleep as a nation:—Ruskin, but he, we say, was cracked on seven lamps; Morris, but he was only an arts-and-crafts man who did not know about the might, majesty, and dominion of the wonderful occult essence called 'Architecture' which is laid on to each of us in a private tap; Mr. March Phillipps, but he thinks architecture should have something to do with life, which it clearly has not; Messrs. Archer, Wells, and Clutton Brock, but they are only literary men; Messrs. Muirhead Bone and Pennell, but they are mere sketchers. Fergusson in his way was continually preaching the doctrine that architects would be 'astonished to find how easy it was to do right, and how difficult to do wrong when expressing the truth only'. Robert Kerr, a forgotten critic of ability, used to say practically the same thing, and so did Emmett, a still more serious writer. These all saw interest in keen life and proud work rather than in the marvellous proportions and exquisite styles of Oxford Street and the Strand. But it can't go on for ever; some day—say, five hundred years hence—architects will have to drop this high-priest business and take to common sense, entering into the life of their time for civilization's sake. Daily experience shows that our own hearts are sick of the vain oblations of style incense to Mumbo Jumbo, while our minds leap at the sight of a building, if haply we may find one, direct, tidy, intelligible. Saying this rather inconsequently reminds me of a *Punch* joke, thirty years old, of a traveller in a French shop. 'Avez-vous perfume de Jockey Club?' 'Yes, sir; we keep all the English smells.' Walk from Bond Street to London Docks and you will see all the English styles, but few healthy buildings confident and smiling.

What would I do? I would have the Institute find a policy in public work for our towns and concentrate on this question of architecture in civilization. Further, I would have all the local bodies follow its lead; and where there are no local bodies, the individual architects, surveyors, builders, and men of goodwill in every town should draw together for the purpose of getting something done in their several towns. The great riddle 'Triglyphs or Crockets?' might be solved by ignoring it and concentrating on structure and the things which matter on which we are agreed. To aim at newness of 'style' would be worse than to aim at oldness of 'style'. Begin just as we are, and taking it all for granted let the leading idea of fit and reasonable building for life's sake and the city's sake gradually become the centre of our thoughts and effort; thus we might turn the corner of style anarchy by concentrating on our agreements.

The Institute should become a centre of effort for better town life—that is its proper business; and it should enter into relations with political economists, publicists, and politicians, and find out what they think (if anything!) about civilization. We should try to get into touch with engineers and lead them to be practical and scientific, and to give up their love for squalor and wriggles; to get them to be patriotic, and not so readily let themselves out to further spoil our towns. Engineers might be told that in Switzerland, for instance, engineering is scientific and not a fumbling jumble of muddle, like our railways with their regular system of haphazard. We architects may beat on our own breasts, but we cannot therefore swallow so-called science whole. The science of mere dividend hunting has to give way to a science of service. Properly speaking, of course, architecture and engineering are closely related, and if we could persuade the engineers to be scientific they might, in turn, get us to be truly artistic and do our work 'just so'. Thus there might be a reasonable drawing together on the common ground of the desire to build up a fine type of English civilization. The things I have mentioned may be looked upon as preliminaries to architecture rather than that wonderful and illusive thing itself; but that does not matter, for these aesthetic altitudes cannot be brought to a clear statement, and it is desirable for us to avoid conflict on poetic, political, or religious theories, and to concentrate on points where there might be hope of attaining some degree of working agreement for our job. If it is said that such commonplaces as I deal with are obvious and do not call for statement, I answer again, Look at the streets! How can such agreement as there is, or may be, on matters of importance to our whole national character as a keen and effective people be turned into stone and brick? that is the question. What can we do the better to bring out our true genius, which I am confident is about the best in the world?

Now, at the end I want to set down some definite propositions which sum up what I would say:

1. It is desirable to bring about some expression of agreement as to facts which would be generally admitted, and which might serve as a basis for our judgement and criticism. Agreement is a necessary preliminary to development.

2. Many things on which we are agreed are not made the basis of an understandable criticism: such points are fitness for function, soundness of structure, economy of means to ends, the need for light, and for easy access for repairs and cleaning, also for efficiency in chimneys, shop-fronts, skylights, windows, roof construction. We have to

consider the best treatment of concrete structures, and all the questions of stone jointing and preservation, plastering, lime-washing, &c.

3. We have to consider our towns and streets as they are in fact: Edgware Road, Oxford Street, Charing Cross Road. Our disorderly railway stations must be taken for granted no longer; we must improve lamp-posts, drain-ventilators, and railings; all must be made clean, smart, and decent. We must aim at the stricter control of public advertising, at smoke prevention, and at better street cleaning, and help forward all minor improvements.

4. Besides their duty to their several employers, architects must consider the city as a whole, to which each building is a contribution. A modern city should be developing types of building fit for its needs. It may be possible to find in the conception of city order and efficiency a real stimulus to building design which should do something towards lessening the disorderly anarchy of our streets. A suitable architecture, in a word, is an essential element in civilization. Architecture properly understood is largely civilization itself. We should seek to stimulate the interest of all architects in the towns in which they work, and we might get reports from them on those towns as centres of civilization. It is desirable to set up advisory committees on the care and development of all our towns.

5. We must co-operate more with engineers and try to influence the powers which govern us to promulgate a policy on public art; we need a statesmanship at the Institute which shall obtain more recognition of our need of the means of civilization, and we must recognize on

our side that we are ministers of civilization rather than purveyors of whims. This Institute should concentrate on a positive constructive policy, directing its education to the same end of the public welfare: its prize subjects, essays, scholarships, might all be made to work in the same direction to the avoidance of much waste. We must aim at getting something done: it is a question of anarchy or order, of life, of survival. More and more the idea emerges that every art, science, and craft must be a guild or faculty for that matter acting in the public service.

6. We should consider whether the reinstatement of some such officer as the Surveyor-General would help us forward. Up to the first quarter of the nineteenth century some sort of effort was made to get the best men to do important public works; then something happened which I have not quite made out, and the custom was broken. In 1819 the Surveyor-General was not Smirke or Pennethorne or Cockerell, but one Colonel Stephenson. In the latter half of the eighteenth century the Dances were surveyors to the City works and did fine buildings like Newgate and St. Luke's. We need an inquiry as to such offices. If they could be bettered in London it would react on all borough surveyorships in the country.

I want the Institute to make this question of architecture and public life its chief work until our towns become better places to live in—that is, are truly civilized.

Chapter X

Education of the Architect [1]

SUPPOSING this was to be the last of our conferences, I have made some notes on one or two things which have been said, but I shall not attempt any full analysis. Some contradictory views may have come out around the fringes of the subjects, but there has been much agreement at the centre.

I ought perhaps to answer one or two direct questions. I have been asked why I would 'concentrate on structural perfection' and why I do not advance to 'some theory by which to express ideas . . . the science of aesthetics, psychology, and human nature'. Now, because I don't think there can be any agreement on aesthetics and human nature so that they can be taught by this Institute, it does not follow that those things do not interest me profoundly. Indeed it is just because I want a true artistic or human-nature content given to our buildings that I would sweep away the teaching of grandiose bunkum as architectural style. Although good bunkum may be jolly sometimes, I want a due proportion of tenderness, gravity, sweetness, and even dullness. I want the most exquisite poetic beauty, but I do not see how this Institute

[1] Royal Institute of British Architects, 1917.

is to teach how to produce it. Therefore I say train us to practical power, make us great builders and adventurous experimenters, then each of us can supply his own poetry to taste. In fact, looking at Holborn and the Strand as they are, I venture to say it would be a sort of poetry to get rid of sham poetry. One of the most sad wastes of power to which men of goodwill are subject is vain strife about words, especially when pairs of words have been allowed to come into opposition—as faith and works, art and science. There is really no opposition between art and science. Show me your art, as St. James might have said, and I will show you your science. Art is the active side of things, science the contemplative. The most of art is science in operation, and a large part of science is reflection upon art. Properly, only science can be taught, for you cannot teach beyond knowledge, and every fresh activity is a sort of creation. This is art—the works whereby we show our science. It is our false idea that art is a sort of ghost which frightens us off true work. It is just this talk about the styles which leads to—Holborn. I know as well as anybody that conception, style, design are essential requirements in all that men do, from guiding the State to laying out a railway or preaching a sermon, but they cannot be supplied by Act of Parliament or by this Institute. While we have been having these meetings another conference was held, the members of which were eager to assure Mr. Neville Chamberlain that architects were not to be thought of as hairdressers in the styles but as men of power as practical builders. Individuals, unfortunately, may make their way by claiming to be the priests of mystery architecture and talking tall art to

Mrs. Jones, but to do so is a grave injury to the whole body, which must stand on reasonable service. It has, in fact, betrayed us to the caricature of Pecksniff. Modern architects have to deal with very complex and technical matters, the building on congested sites of great hotels, railway stations, factories, business premises, and the like, and for this it is clear to me there must be highly organized scientific training. What are the main divisions into which different faculties might run? There seem to me to be about five: (1) the expert constructor and planner, (2) the finisher and furnisher, (3) the expert in old buildings, (4) the man of business, (5) the country builder and general practitioner. There is no sharp distinction but I think most men gravitate to one or other of these classes or to a combination of two or even three of them, and there is room for high attainment in any one. The first and the last should be the main concern of this Institute. Probably the standard for a time should be that of the general practitioner, but ways must be found to stimulate specialization beyond the minimum course—a point to which I shall return in touching on education.

There has been remarkable agreement in the view that this Institute should take up questions of public welfare in matters relating to building more definitely and constantly, that it is called upon to enter on a large constructive policy, and even to engage in earnest propaganda work. In working for the public interest this Institute would incidentally find a worthy place for itself, but, unless we awake, the new cottages, national housing, and town improvements will be done in the main without us.

The Institute does not fill its part as a trade union

according to modern conceptions. The trades unions have come to occupy a position in the State, functioning publicly, in collective bargaining and making their wills felt in national life. Whenever and however have we architects been willing or able to make our collective will felt? The administrators of public affairs seem to look on us as city-clerk sort of people out for hire, and if we are ever called in to advise it is usually as a mere screen so that they may the better exercise their own will under cover of 'experts'. If the experts do not advise just what the organizers want the advice is contemptuously brushed aside. This Institute has to see to it that in matters of public building policy the advice of architects is not only sought but taken. I was told the other day that the architectural bodies in the United States were acquiring almost too much power—nothing could be done 'without their interference'. Certainly in America there is a growing sense that good building is essential in the great modern State. In regard to this question of public control, I raised the question of the possibility of reviving the Surveyor-Generalship. I have been looking into the origin and suppression of that important office. It appears that Inigo Jones took over part of the functions of the old master-masons to the King, who were the surveyors of royal building works from the early Middle Ages. The Surveyor-Generalship continued till 1813, when James Wyatt, the last architect to hold the office, died. He had been appointed in 1796, when he succeeded Chambers. Wyatt was 'Surveyor-General and Comptroller of His Majesty's Office of Works'—that is, I suppose, the Civil Service chief, and what we now call the Permanent

Secretary. On some reconstitution the architect was left out.[1] It seems to me that it would be quite reasonable to aim at putting an architect again in control of the Office of Works.

Coming to educational policy, the Institute's business is with civilization, town improvement, national housing, quality in building, cottage types, the preservation of historical buildings, better public memorials, and a public policy of betterment all round. At present individual architects are at the mercy of vulgar accidents, such as having a flow of dinner-talk, or being in with a business syndicate, or knowing a lord. This Institute has to win a place for the ablest building directors considered as essential ministers of civilization, and to see to it that public works are done in a proper way. To do this they must enter on a large and consistent educational policy. We have been educated long enough as purveyors of whims, ecclesiastical and domestic; our education must be recast in the public service.

The Institute should become a centre of stimulating life; we should try to draw together publicists, thinkers, economists, critics, town and trade union officials, and the masters of the City Guilds, in an effort to get something done in bettering our towns: it is not only our duty to lead, it is our business. All our own powers should be reconsidered from the same point of view of a public

[1] A warrant for the appointment of Inigo Jones is in the British Museum (Add. 5755). The last Surveyor-General was Sir B. C. Stephenson, and the office ceased about 1834. After this Mr. H. H. Steward was appointed Surveyor. The Board of Works was constituted in 1851; previously H.M. Office of Works dealt with Crown properties.

policy. Our committees need new instructions, our scholarships should be reshaped, and our whole educational requirements need to be penetrated by a spirit of activity. We need an architectural statesmanship in a campaign for civilization. More and more this powerful body is being left isolated as an architects' remuneration society because it does not come out and teach and do public work. Its proper field of activity is enormous: it is a local society for London, a national society, and a society representing the Commonwealth all in one.

Education needs more than machinery; it needs enthusiasm. We require some literature which should bring the minds of young students into contact with larger ideas than 'shop' and the passing of examinations. We should make Wren a patron saint, for Wren was a great Englishman, and in all he did worked for England.

We have, in the liberal prize endowments of the Institute and in the original essay which forms a part of the matter examined, valuable means for opening up special interests. And here I would say that the essays seem to me to have been a marked success. A fault is that custom compels us to mark poor ones too highly, but they could be improved to almost any extent by rigorously rejecting those which are only compiled from text-books. Mr. Innocent says, in the preface to his book on traditional building construction (the most valuable piece of such work which has been published for years), that the line of study was undertaken in connexion with the Institute examinations. Mr. Weir reminded us of some excellent thoughts on education, and Sir T. Jackson's idea of a real school of architecture, where the young craftsman, builder, and architect would work together, seemed to me convincing common sense. In the excellent School of Building at Brixton we have, I am glad to suppose, a near approximation to the kind, and I was delighted to hear from a speaker at an earlier Conference that the type was to be extended.

We architects are a part of life. Only three nights ago I dreamed I met an old architect whom I reverence [Philip Webb, in fact]. And I was speaking about this business to him in my dream, and he said, 'There is no going beneath the ground plane'. As in dreams we think things are wonderful, I thought, 'What an amazing phrase! That sums up the whole business; and in the most perfect form it crystallizes all architectural wisdom.' I knew he meant you cannot go outside the stream; you are yourself part of the stream; you cannot go outside environment; you yourself are conditioned by it. It is the deadness of our town life which produces the deadness of our architecture: the unutterable deadness which has come over English cities and villages in the last forty years, the stagnation and daily dying of the towns up and down the country. I was surprised about three weeks ago at seeing an article by a hardened political economist—a man whose name we do not mention here—who managed to miss his train on a drizzly day at Oldham, and he had to hang about the station for an hour. And in that hour something happened to him. Having nothing else to do, he began to think. And that political economist saw Oldham, and it came home to him that that was England; that there were dozens and hundreds of these Oldhams all over England, and that all England is becoming more and more like

Oldham. Now, until we can heighten the life of such towns, and get them to rebuild themselves, and put themselves into order, and clean themselves, nothing will happen to architects or to anybody else. But in the rebuilding of our towns, if we could set about it, we might find some vitalizing principle in our architecture. If we can begin to live in our towns we shall instantly again have live architecture in our midst. I remember myself how beautiful were the towns throughout England fifty years ago. In the little town in which I lived no vulgarity had touched it at that time; it was a thing which had grown; it was a work of art and beauty, a work which Turner would have painted. But now it is wrapped round with railways, and exploited and miserified, and the shops have been turned into emporiums for picture postcards. It is that which conditions our architecture. Until the spring of life bursts out in our towns, what does any architecture matter? Nothing at all until more public work gives us a new tradition. We have, in the meantime, merely to satisfy the whims of generously minded employers, and until we have a life independent of that hanging-on, no architecture is possible. In fact, one of the most important things in modern architecture is the Art of Dining Out.

Chapter XI

Education for Appreciation or for Production? [1]

THE proposition of this little paper is that English education, as traditionally developed and guided from the old Universities, is not directed to production and to action. It is an education in appreciation and in a knowledge of what has been written. It is by its very nature retrospective, and at its best it is introspective —the proper introduction to a life of contemplation. It may be developed to so fine a point of 'pure scholarship' and elegant criticism as to become sterilizing and destructive. This type of education has become an English 'ceremonial institution'. It was the great class badge and the foundation for the old Civil Service and a Parliamentary career. At its worst (and that was very bad) it was an education in 'side', 'bluff', and voice production; its inward unrealized function was to provide a myth of superiority to those who could pay. Since mail went out of fashion it became the defensive armour of a class. At its most acute point it seems to have aimed at inducing ignorance of everything but the writing of sham Latin verse and prose. At its reformed broadest it seems to propose some knowledge of languages, history, mathematics,

[1] Education Conference, Southport, 1919.

and 'pure' science, with some understanding of what has been said in literature and philosophy. The aim of even Matthew Arnold was 'culture', the being able 'to move freely in the realm of ideas'. This is doubtless good enough in its way—one way—but we cannot all take the veil and retire from the often rough productive work of the world. Such education is very nice and proper, and it may be that this type, improved and amended, may be preserved as leading up to one kind of human training—the department of archaeological scholarship and historical culture.

The appreciation of the highest, which it offers, is of a limited and back-looking kind. Even for this restricted ground, who but the producer really understands production? Who understands a cathedral—the architect or a tourist? Who is musical, the composer or the concert-goer? Who is athletic, the player or the crowd? 'And so of other arts,' as Plato would say, who except he who practises them can truly appreciate what they are and mean? The spectator of football and concerts does evidently appreciate those arts in some way, but according to the sliding scale of his technical knowledge and understanding sympathy may readily pass into mere amusement or bemusement. All right appreciation, I feel, must be closely related to the discipline of productiveness, or it cannot long remain a free delight. This free delight is of the nature of intoxication. Still, as I say, I am willing to think that a narrow, academical circle might be a preserve for the pure scholars of past productions, blind to all but books and sterile for their learning's sake. The old distinction between the active and contemplative lives was sound if it is understood that we cannot afford too many contemplators.

It is a different matter when we turn from such cloistered colleges to the world of labour, adventure, and invention, where most men have to live their lives and give their contribution to society. For this other, and necessarily vastly larger world, a very different type of education is needed than that in which the 'humanities' are identified with dreaming and divorced from doing. The control by academical scholars of the vast field of modern education must be loosened, for they start with an avowed doubt of all vocational education except that for their own narrow vocation of letters conceived in an historical spirit. General education has to be re-thought out as the preparation for various vocations, each of which is as cultural in its own way (more or less, and in some cases much more) as the vocation of scholarship. Education should be an apprenticeship to life and service, and workers will have to educate their would-be instructors to the knowledge that there are diversities of culture by the very nature of things. The universe is far greater than the university. As a matter of fact, Oxford and Cambridge were developed as schools for clergy. They are vocational schools of a very narrow kind. As most men have to do work, our education has to be re-oriented towards the active life. Production will carry, unconsciously within itself, the due proportion of high appreciation, and general culture will none the less be there, because it is attached to many different main stems. No one can do any worthy thing well but that he may thereby become a man, and the true end of culture is to make men.

The old type of education has gone dangerously far to create a distaste for work by its presupposition that culture was alone to be found in books. To counteract this modern disease of thought we shall need some very definite new teaching of a religious kind, which will reverence, and even worship, the great precedent necessity of labour. If any man will be a saint, let him dig or make. We must begin with the spirit; we have to light up a flame of desire to serve in all ways of human work. We should first of all meet on some ground common to all Englishmen ('Sirs, ye be brethren'), and elementary education should become a folk training which should give all alike a traditional lore—a British Bible.

Beyond this point education and production need to be brought together in new types of apprenticeship. It is absurd to aim at merely abstract and grammatical preparation until the age of twenty or thirty. Even for those who prefer to read books, the scholarship university should be a research workshop. The vocational ideal in education is not only a theory which would apply to a commercial and industrial people, but it would rationalize and make human the 'humanities' themselves. If we would seriously set about building up a productive epoch, we must begin by training and tempering the national mind, suggesting a strong desire for a noble type of life, which shall not only use the words of civilization, but produce all the works thereof as well. We must consciously aim at bringing in a great epoch, a period of culmination which will become historical. With such an idea and intensive training, we might in a single generation become quite a friendly, humanized, and civilized people. We must get it understood that work is not necessarily slavery. Such a view could only have been induced by our great misleaders, 'philosophers' and 'political economists', when they took the will to work for granted. Goodness knows that will is so much a part of the springs of life that it has been hard to chill it, but it has been chilled. We must consciously aim at the production and perfection of every kind of reasonable and noble workmanship, from making bread and boots to houses and cities. Drama, music, architecture, are not the result of chance gusts of inspiration blowing where they will, but they are necessarily produced where a strong tide of life is flowing.

PS.—Since writing this I have seen an article in the *Hibbert Journal* (Oct. 1918) entitled 'A New Birth for Education', by Professor Caldwell, writing from Canada, with which I am in enthusiastic agreement. [Later again I have been delighted to find Mr. Wells suggesting the formation of a British Bible.]

Chapter XII

Apprenticeship and Education [1]

ALL I have to say is an amplification of the idea that all education should be apprenticeship, and all apprenticeship should be education. Education has become, in the thoughts of many, far too much a mere abstract grammar, and far too bookish. This bookish method has invaded even art education. Instead of learning directly how to draw in the simplest and yet surest way, one is supposed to learn first all about drawing in various subdivisions and artificial compartments, as freehand drawing, model drawing, perspective drawing, life drawing, and the like. Of course, it may be convenient to divide up a big subject like drawing into firstly, secondly, and thirdly, and the names freehand, model, shaded drawing from the cast and the rest are as serviceable as any others, if it can be only made clear in the student's mind that they are but many words for the one thing, drawing, and that the end of drawing is to represent an object or to convey an idea not according to this or any other classification, but in the most effective way possible. Too elaborate approaches to a practical subject, a form of *gymnastic* like drawing, are very wasteful of time and very

[1] International Conference on Drawing, South Kensington, 1910.

destructive of confidence. It is as if one had to learn all about swimming under hydrostatics and mechanics before entering the water.

The great end is production, the great thing is the trade, the craft, and sufficient culture can be hung up to any sufficient trade. The ordinary University course in England is really, and has been developed historically as, a preparation for the vocations of being a landed proprietor or a clerk in orders. Primarily it was an apprenticeship to the callings depending on letters; its whole course and degrees are parallel to the years of apprenticeship, and to the taking of the mastership in any of the old callings regulated by guilds, but those callings provided also other forms of education. A University, indeed, is a Guild of Letters, and only one of several guilds. Although a certain amount of differentiation is found in University courses for those who are to follow medicine, law, and the like, men who are to practise arts, as painters, sculptors, musicians, builders, are not likely to go through such a course without injury to their force and productive gifts. What is wanted is a rational recognition of the fact that as life is a many-sided thing, so education must have many forms. When a true form of universal education comes, the principal activities of life will have to be grouped into several divisions, faculties, or guilds, and then, I have no doubt, each typical faculty will make rules for proper education and apprenticeship in the given form of life, thus approximating once again to the old guild system. The unit for regulating education is properly, it seems to me, the organized art or craft, that is to say, its Guild. All proper education is the opening up of a necessary and beneficent life occupation, and the exercise of such a calling furnishes the sanest and largest education in life itself.

Drawing is best taught along with apprenticeship to a craft, or otherwise it becomes so generalized that it is difficult for the ordinary student to see its application, and it becomes only a 'subject'. In thus generalizing it into a grammar apart from its application, the most valuable parts of the teaching of drawing have often been forgotten. These most valuable parts are, I consider, (1) the bringing before the student fine material on which he forms his mind; (2) the unconscious absorption of facts not only as to the shape of man, but fine ornamental forms, letters, heraldry, symbols, &c.; (3) the collection of examples for use, so that if one wants a vine, a rose, a ship, or a stag, there is a study of it already laid up for reference. The old masters drew with this object, and that is why their drawings were treasured and handed on. Modern masters, like Alfred Stevens or Burne-Jones, also drew in this way to store up observations, but how late in the day the idea comes to most students that their studies are not (for example) mere 'Life drawings', but observations of attitude and action forming so much valuable stock-in-trade! These supplementary purposes of learning drawing have been, I think, so much forgotten because drawing has been divided off from the crafts, even from the craft of painting, and I, for my part, think that all advanced drawing should be carried on in association with the learning of a craft, be it carpentry or sculpture; nothing else makes it sufficiently real and vital: a cabinet-maker or silver-worker, in learning to draw, should accumulate quite a museum of examples.

I

Many approaches to the apprenticeship ideal are being made, I hope, but with the statistical details I do not propose to attempt to deal, and I confine myself only to the idea. The great object of specific education seems to me the acquisition of a worthy craft by which to live. There is quite enough which belongs to, or can be properly associated with, all such callings to open out a way to raise up diverse forms of culture; the rest is converse and commerce with nature, men, and books. Much of the book education of the present time is an elaborate apology for our ignorance of all but print.

Chapter XIII

The Need for Beauty [1]

*W*hat is *Art*, and what is Beauty, that communities should bother about them at all?

Art is many-sided and manifold: it is not only a question of high genius; that is only the crest of a great wave rising from gifted peoples, and without the flood of common art you cannot have the crest of genius. This common art, which is the thing of importance (as the other will form itself out of it), is concerned with all the routine things of life—laying the breakfast table and cleaning the door-steps of our houses, tidying up our railway stations, and lighting the High Streets of our towns.

Too much writing about art, over-splashed with purple and dazzling with paradox, seems to have entirely confused ordinary people. When you have divided up this common principle of Life in Work into Fine Art, Decorative Art, Architectural Art, Art at the Mayfair Galleries and 'the Art of Mr. Smith', the next step is to forget the whole business, as being too technical, or rather to turn it over to specialists, who say they know all about it.

[1] Civic Arts Society, 1916.

In much the same way, Beauty has been ground to dust in contradictory theories of Aesthetics. Indeed, some books on this simplest, sweetest thing, Beauty, must make the animals glad that they have not learnt to read. Beauty, like breathing, is solved by doing it, not by this ever-lasting argument. Might I venture, as an illustration, to say that St. James must have found a similar difficulty with over-systematic discussions about Faith. 'What I mean by Faith'—he seems to say in a famous passage—'is—is everything.' That, too, is what I mean by Art—everything that was ever rightly done or made. By Art we live and move and have our being. If we have not Art, we shall just perish for ever! Art is cleanliness, tidiness, order, gaiety, serenity, mastery, the right way of doing right things. The civic arts are the arts of civilization. The arts of civilization are civilization itself.

Even if Art enters into all things made and done, I should not worry you about it if it were only a matter of shapes and colours and skill, but it is much more than all these. Beauty is a necessary function of fitness; Beauty is the smile of Health, and it is one of the few great things which sustain the spirit of communities. In the days before us, we shall need to make use of all the sources of power we can draw on—Historical Continuity, Pride of Race, National Spirit, Love of Home, and Civic Patriotism. The civic arts mean pride and strength, more life and more to love. That country must be greatest which has the most to love. Without refreshment of spirit the people must become brittle, wither and fail. Beauty is the 'substance' of things done, as faith is the substance of things hoped for.

We have heaps of Teachers, Philosophers, Politicians, and Economists, but none that I hear of seems to understand that no nation can last without Beauty.

Chapter XIV

What shall we call Beautiful? [1]

A PRACTICAL VIEW OF AESTHETICS [2]

A fool sees not the same tree that a wise man sees.—BLAKE.

ALL the questions about sight and delight are extremely difficult. It is a trite truth that we have never really seen a thing, a tree, for instance, but only partial aspects of many trees. Even these partial aspects are conditioned by our relations in time and space. They are images which arise between the object, tree, and you, the observer. If, for instance, the seasons were hurried up and became a thousand times quicker, we

---

[1] *Hibbert Journal*, 1918.

[2] We may best get a general statement on aesthetics from the excellent article in the *Encyclopaedia Britannica*. In its original Greek form it means what has to do with sense perception as a source of knowledge. Its limitation to that part of our sense perceptions which we know as the contemplative enjoyment of beauty is due to A. G. Baumgarten. . . . By pure contemplation is to be understood that manner of regarding objects of sense perception, and more particularly sights and sounds, which is entirely motived by the pleasure of the act itself. . . . Aesthetic pleasure is pure enjoyment. . . . Aesthetic enjoyment is clearly marked off from practical life. . . . It seeks one or more regulative principles which may help us to distinguish a real from an apparent aesthetic value, and to set the higher and more perfect illustrations of beauty above the lower and less perfect.

should see our tree bud, spread out its leaves, and fade in an afternoon—it would gush out like a fountain into green and be gone. It is changing all the time now, but we do not see it. Again, if it were magnified several thousand times, its solidity would dissolve into a vague fog form. Its colour, green, is partly in the leaves, partly in the light, but mostly in our eyes. What, apart from our ways of apprehending it, can a tree be, the thing in itself? All we know of it is struck out by the contact of a 'thing' and our senses. 'Tree' is not objective or subjective.

Turning from such 'material' and 'tangible' objects to our generalized ideas on the aspects which possess the qualities that we call Beauty, we find that the phenomena are conditioned by a great number of still more complex and confusing factors. They involve many questions in regard to what we see, what we think we see, when we see, and who does the seeing. Doubtless the executioner thought of his fine new rack, 'That is a beauty'; but what did the executee think?

Beauty, we may at least say, is not objective or subjective: it arises in our contemplation of exciting objects. Mr. Clive Bell says that what is common to beautiful works of art is 'significant form', but does not sufficiently explain of what the forms are to be significant. Miss Jane Harrison would amend it to emotional, but it is not clear as to who is to feel the emotion or what kind it should be. In London at this minute, who is the instructed and competent observer whom we will trust to tell us about the emotional significance of form?

The best corrective I know to such opinions is Mr. A. J. Balfour's 'Criticism of Beauty', although it seems to me a little disappointing in stopping short of expressing positive views. He makes it clear, however, that what pleases one age and one stage of culture does not necessarily please another, and that at this time there is no agreement between competent observers. Was there ever, indeed, so great anarchy? Mr. Balfour a while plays with the subject, and leaves it in the air: he demonstrates that nothing can be proved of beauty; yet nevertheless it moves. Having shown that there is no agreement as to what people think beautiful, a philosopher might at least have made his own attempt to put a valuable content into the word. Not so did Plato conduct his argument in his 'Criticism of Justice', and exactly the same treatment might be applied to every valuable word in the dictionary if the philosopher cared. What is Justice? What is Liberty? What is Truth? What is Honour? Honour at least is a notion which is good for Boy Scouts. I foresee a time when we shall have to write every second word in 'quotes'. At the end, however, Mr. Balfour finely says that our admiration should be even as our loves, which I suppose implies that we *should* admire the highest when we see it. Yet he objects that in much of Ruskin's work 'aesthetics, theology, and morals are inextricably intertwined', and then admits for himself 'some mystical reference to first and final causes'. Why, then, was Ruskin wrong in considering the question as a complete man rather than as one who merely wanted his nerves art-tickled?

The aesthetic problem is wrongly set out. To the question, 'What gives man aesthetic delight?' there is no general answer. The question must be, 'What should give him aesthetic delight here and now?' To which the prompt answer is, 'That which it is good for him and for the society in which he lives to think beautiful.' That which it is good for people to think Justice *is* Justice. It is as silly and dangerous to set up a theory of enjoyment in art without inquiry as to where it will lead, as to set up a science of the delights of drugs and drams. Plato saw all that. Indeed, this aesthetic of art as enjoyment is as thin as a theory of manners apart from conduct—it is mere superficial etiquette. With its concern with 'taste', it is no better than a cookery book. Aesthetic delight in drinks, even in food, is dangerously subject to disease; and un-related aesthetic delight in art leads straight to the plague and destruction. A nervous, irritated, city-dwelling gener-ation is especially, of course, subject to such aesthetic diseases. Most of our artists are trained in abstract 'Art', without any ballasting teaching as to what it is all about. They pass through the forcing-houses of competitive schools and exhibitions, and are maddened by ignorant writers who have to provide penny lines in the half-penny press. Our men have splendid ability and earnest-ness, but society, after having trained them for a time, refuses to employ them in any rational way and leaves them to live by their wits. Is there any wonder that art, thus acquired and practised, sometimes turns sour and makes the artist see emerald green?

There is in fact a brown-bread and dewy-morning ideal of beauty, and a late champagne-supper ideal. Who could say which was the right one were it not for Necessity's 'You must'? We have to love the health ideal, or cease to exist. Necessity is not only the Mother of Invention, but of all the other children too. At least it is certain that some

of the common people must be persuaded that plain food
and normal health are beautiful, or we could not carry
on; and it is really a mistake of the late-supper gentry to
say so much about their raptures. Necessity forces on us
the view that—Beauty is the expression of health. There
was a Greek proverb quoted by Plato with strong
approval thus: 'That is, and ever will be, the best of
sayings, that *the useful is the noble and the hurtful is the base.*'

We so readily assume that our customs of looking
through crowded collections of oil-paintings in paltry
gilt frames once a year, and of listening to concert-hall
music being 'performed' once a month, are in the very
nature of the cosmic order, that it may be hard to imagine
extensions of aesthetic rapture beyond the orbit of our
experience. However, may I put the case for what I will
call a Smell Concert? You are to imagine a large domical
hall, with circling plush seats and the 'play of lights',
palms, and all that; then scent fountains gush forth
and incense from swaying censers, first thin and fine, then
full gales of oriental spicery . . . and so on; fill out the
brilliant occasion from the daily press. Would not this be
aesthetic? Why should we recoil from it as trivial and
enervating, as luxury without life, if the aesthetic account
of art-thrills is valid and right?

The whole theory of Fine Art and aesthetic delights
apart from purposes and ends had as distinct an historical
birth-time as the modern doctrine of the Will to Power.
Aristotle, the first of those who knew in physics, was
affected in the arts by the current thought of the Hellenistic decadence which, in a slow, lovely decline, had
been going on for a century. The art history of his time

had been precisely the emergence of a free and luxurious art practised for delight: yet, notwithstanding, it is a marvel how justly and sternly the great master thought on the matter; his one mistake seems to have been to consider free delight in the arts at all. It left just enough room for the flies to settle on. Plato refused to allow any such nonsense.

It is one of Mr. Balfour's ideas that the essentials of art can best be studied in music, as there it can most readily be 'isolated from utility'—this is the old desire of watertighting phenomena; the wish to study the life of the fish out of the water. First, the experts split off 'art' from work and utility, and then they split off 'fine art' from commoner stuff, and then they are ready for aesthetics, by isolating their emotions of delight. Even the first step, the isolation from work of an element called art, is fatal to both work and art—it is isolating life from the body. It is, I believe, flatly opposed to reason and right that the art which can be most completely isolated from service—this is said to be music—can best be questioned for the constant characteristics of art. Just the reverse is true: first examine facts where art is inseparable from service; there you will find plain data for a just theory in obscurer regions. But is music essentially a free art, any more than the rest? What assumptions philosophers will swallow! Music was developed, as a matter of fact, as an emotional stimulus to practical ends: as work stimulus, war stimulus, religious stimulus, and national stimulus. Is not this 'utility'? The obvious fact is that the springs of music are with life, work, and purpose, and this 'isolating' of it into a 'fine art' has dried the sources up. I was glad later to find that here I had been in agreement with the view expressed by A. Della Seta in his important *Religion and Art* (1914). Don't the connoisseurs really know that all the music we can hear now is an echo and that Pan is sleeping? Bring back music to noble use; it will quickly revive and we shall have a national art once more. 'Virtue is the strong stem of human nature, and music is the blossoming of virtue' (Confucius).

As with the man who inquired whether he had yet attained wisdom, so with anxiety about enjoying beauty, the answer must ever be, 'It might have been, if you had not thought about it.' Beauty has to come by the way.

Fine art has been differentiated from what I shall call work-art, less because of its status than because Aristotle, writing at the time when such ideas were being worked out towards their doom, thought that certain acts were free of utility. Architecture was not a 'fine art' because it was too much conditioned by needs. Croce, however, is disposed, I think rightly, to deny the old-fashioned distinction altogether.

Fine art equals free art; but even so it is only as free as language, it is not free to be nonsensical or to spread disease. This freer art (I cannot admit free) is best conceived, indeed, as another form of language, and we might almost say that fine art equals speech art. From the beginning (whenever that was) men practised different means of communication. Speech, writing, acting, dancing, music, painting, sculpture are all means of telling, informing, preaching. Music will say some valuable things which common talking will not. It is not an artificial thing, it was from the beginning. Then, again, writing and painting are closely related, and it is not usually realized that painting is the older art. Writing was short-hand painting, and the letters were 'pictographs'.

Drawing, painting, and sculpture will say many things much more powerfully and accurately than all the talk-ing; they are a necessary means of communication, and were so from the earliest times. Like the other languages of words and music, they may in all sorts of ways say all sorts of things. They may be immature but have true strength and nobility, or they may be dazzlingly clever yet silly and weakening, just like a printed book. A well-painted picture or a clever piece of music may form a centre of health or a culture of disease. How shall we know? For one thing, we must base our judgement on wider ground than our individual likings and amuse-ment; all must be judged as for the community. Artists, like everybody else, live by common service; they are cooked for and clothed, and laundresses do their washing. They, too, must be persuaded to work for the common good in return.

Art is many things—service, record, and stimulus: it is not only a question of genius; without the basis of com-mon art you cannot have the apex of genius. This common art, which is the thing of importance—as freer arts will be formed out of it—is concerned with all the ordinary things of life.

Modern writers try to separate the emotional aspects from the bases which are their necessary support, but in its history the word Art has meant Workmanship. The outward expression of work-art cannot be separated from a residuum of merely brute labour without beating down labour to slavery and giving over free art to speedy disease and dissolution. Writers on aesthetics have not sufficiently recognized that Art is *service* before it is delight; it is *labour* as well as emotion; it is *substance* as well as expression. What they say is here and there true enough in its way, but it is a way that leads to destruction; it is concerned with appearances rather than conduct. For philosophers seriously to discuss the pure lyricism of Art can only help to turn it towards hysteria. Beauty is the flowering of labour and service. There are things so beautiful, indeed, that you must always pretend you don't see them, and notice them out of the corner of your eye, as you see a linnet on a nest.

Modern aesthetic thinkers—saving for some sectional inquiries—fall into much the same fallacy as do the economists of supposing that 'we are the people'. Is it not at once obvious that a doctrine of beauty common to Esquimaux and Hottentots, Greeks, Mediaevals, and ourselves, cannot be 'formulated'? What they really have in mind, for the most part, is a theory suitable for modern picture exhibitions and the music of the Queen's Hall. In the main it is aesthetics for dealers—a philosophy for Piccadilly and Regent Street.

The Italian thinker, Benedetto Croce, has perhaps made the most mark of recent writers on aesthetics in his series of works dealing with the 'Philosophy of the Spirit'. He conceives of the Spirit acting through three or four vital activities, by the Will, by Logic and Science, and by Aesthetic Appreciation. In these the Spirit moves by intuition, Beauty being 'pure lyricism'.

This view has been adopted by Mr. Clutton-Brock in *The Ultimate Belief* (1916), a very interesting little book. Here we are told of right, truth, and beauty that:

'These three desires and these alone are desires of the Spirit; and they differ from all our other desires in that they are to be pursued for their own sake.' (p. 20)

'Unless I value truth for its own sake, I cannot discover truth. Unless I value beauty for its own sake, I cannot see or hear or in any way experience beauty.' (p. 27)

'We exercise an aesthetic judgement about all things which we know to be different from our moral or intellectual judgements.' (p. 65)

'Aesthetic value is distinct in itself from practical value.' (p. 69)

This seems so nearly a return to the German doctrine of Art for Art's sake as to make me very doubtful, or rather to make me sure in opposition to the statement; yet the author's intentions are obviously most trustworthy, and it is important that something very like the doctrine should be got into the minds of the people. Truly the activities of the Spirit must flow out in goodness, in the search for truth and the apprehension of beauty. As a result of system-making, however, Mr. Clutton-Brock seems to me to be led into over-statement. For example:

'The aesthetic value can be clearly distinguished from the value of utility. We have an extreme aesthetic value for some things, such as music, which have no utility, nor have they any moral or intellectual value.' (p. 69)

This is as arguable as anything else, but the theory will in practice be found a robe which will cover curiously free forms of Art, and will be taken to sanction even 'Blastism'.

Did Mr. Clutton-Brock not feel doubts when Croce cleared the ground of Plato, Ruskin, and Tolstoy? The idea that our faculties should be developed in the good, the true, and the beautiful is, of course, as sound as old; but the activity towards Beauty should rather be conceived as directed to service, production, creation, than to aesthetic enjoyment or contemplation. The view is too static—'possessive rather than creative'. Then, the doctrine of free activity is, I believe, bad for Art itself, whose strength is in service: 'free activity' is a 'heady wine', as Lord Roberts said of 'the Will to Power'. Approaching the subject on my lines, I seem to see our dear mistake of watertighting; and I do not even feel sure that the three categories must be exhaustive. The scheme is a little like the old question, 'Animal, vegetable, or mineral?' Are not the desires towards activity and creative energy and the regulative impulses manifestations of Spirit? The three are either too few or too many. Or it should be added—these three are one. Croce, indeed, seems to incline to allow a fourth division, the economic. Mr. Clutton-Brock, I should say, gives all I want if he would allow one of his phrases to be extended all round: speaking of knowledge, he says, 'without it the moral activity loses its sense of direction'. I want to add of the aesthetic activity that, without like supervision, it loses its sense of direction. It is the direction that counts in the long run. No one has ever proved that any form of aesthetic activity has more right to a free existence than the enjoyment of snuff-taking, or gaming, which are also modes of aesthetic enjoyment.

The search for knowledge is no more a 'free activity'

than delight in beauty; the subject matter of science, as Tolstoy said, being infinite, the searcher must select. Science has selected poison gas. All 'facts' are not truths; there is a scale of values.

Recently, new material on the origins of Art has been brought to light—or rather, new light has been brought to old material—in caves occupied by prehistoric peoples, the rock roofs of which are covered by forceful paintings, tens of thousands of years old, of animals of the chase. The general view is that they were painted for magical purposes rather than for enjoyment. Then Capart, in an excellent study of the earliest Egyptian Art, showed that even patterns had quite a different origin from 'the futile pleasure in decoration'. Again, Della Seta, in considering Art as it developed historically, comes to the conclusion that there was little or no 'free activity' about it: rather was it religious, magical, and utilitarian, as Stone-Age men conceived utility:—

'Art profane in origin, born to satisfy the aesthetic taste which seeks for expression rather than for the utility of its products, even if this be a spiritual utility, is inconceivable, and has never existed.'

Of music he says:—

'No branch of art has so detached itself from its utilitarian character.'

To one, however, who holds that all sound work is Art, it is manifestly impossible to accept Della Seta's identification of Art with religion: that is, with religion as ordinarily conceived; I, as may be evident, hold that good work

K

is a prime factor in right religion. His treatise, however, is an excellent account of Art as it has existed in fact. A still more rigorous examination of the origins of some phases of Art has lately been published by Professor Ridgeway (*The Drama*, &c., 1916). Mankind sought to win the favour of the dead by offerings and dances, and 'tragedy arose out of these dramatic dances'. Writers, instead of seeking for the origin of the drama by the historical method, have approached 'from the *a priori* standpoint of pure aesthetics. . . . The study of art is almost invariably based on *a priori* assumptions'.

It may now be held as proved that Art was everywhere developed for what were supposed to be utilitarian purposes. Yet Croce and most of the writers on aesthetics assume that the appreciation of art is mainly a matter of a special intuitive 'feeling'. All that should be admitted is the possibility, under conditions, of some little aesthetic feeling. Our judgement acts so quickly in summing up a complex subject matter, that it may seem an intuition, but it is a very extended intuition. This 'feeling' for Art is, so to say, the Art-conscience, and has to be instructed by reason and experience. Beauty can only be thought of as an 'aesthetic' whole for purposes of 'philosophy'! Practically and truly, it is something quite different. Beauty is not the thing in itself, but the idea of beauty arises in us; 'us' being infinitely varying individuals. The modern feeling for beauty in Art, as it exists in any given case, is likely to include perception and estimates of:

(1) Service value, worth, desirability. (2) Fitness for purpose. (3) Skill of the maker. (4) Economy of means to ends, concentration, intensity. (5) Completeness, order,

unity, magnitude. (6) Insight into essential character. (7) Freshness, health, life, growth, movement. (8) Sympathy with the mind of the maker, approval, wonder. (9) Religious and patriotic values, as liking our own people and landscape. (10) Personal associations, ownership, &c. (11) Reputation—the same work, when proved to be by Michael Angelo, seems better than when it was thought to be by Vasari. (12) Relation to historical development —very important: an excellent 'modern Gothic' church is worthless. (13) Scarcity and other accidents, the fashion of the moment, strangeness, &c. (14) Then there are factors like pleasure in form relations and colour, a sense of rhythm and 'lyricism'. I have been told by visitors to Japan that the people seem to possess a rhythmical sense lost by Western people; they even walk rhythmically. I suppose, however, that this is a natural expression of race health. Again, there seems to be a natural delight in imitation and the awaking of recollection. (15) Further, there are other ideas of luxury, sex-attraction, and all sorts of borderlands, intoxications, diseases, and perversions. There is also, doubtless, some sediment of the ancient feeling of the magic of Art.

Through such a labyrinth the modern man has to see his way in arriving at his aesthetic judgements. Our appreciation of any work of Art can hardly be anything else than the sum of stimulus to us resulting from such factors as these, which come to us as understanding, contentment, approval, wonder. Beauty may be sought as an absolute, but it is always found as the resultant of a group of relations. Our sense of beauty is the overflow of delight from that which we think lovable. In free aesthetics the delight may either be healthy or harmful. We have to see to it that what we decide to call beauty is health-giving. What I elect to call beautiful is my reading in work of evidence that the people producing it were healthy all round and noble. I have not proved my case, of course; what case is ever proved? But I have suggested that it is not necessary to believe the aesthetic writers—at least, I have shown that I do not believe much of them myself.

Aesthetic 'institutions' are not in any case the frank desires of a child; they are the rapid judgements of an experienced man. As in a conversation our instant answer leaps out from the very sum of ourselves, our temperament, knowledge, and convictions; so in the argument before any work of Art our responses spring from no special aesthetic faculty, but from all our loves and loathings. The current theories of aesthetics have been elaborated and re-elaborated, cycle on epicycle, for the most part by word-philosophers. I don't suppose that Herr Baumgarten had any special knowledge of the laws of craftsmanship; his theories were doubtless argued down from the pure idea. We have perhaps not sufficiently recognized how much of German thinking is frankly of the nature of a scholastic thesis.

Ruskin speaks of the 'mental expression' of Art, and this is much the best thing to look for. Art is a language not a grimace.

Morris, again, says of Ruskin:

'Ethical and political considerations have never been absent from his criticism of art; and in my opinion it is just this part of his work which has had the most enduring and beneficent effect. . . . Ruskin has let a flood of daylight into the cloud of sham technical twaddle which was once the whole substance of art criticism.'

Morris wrote this towards the end of his life; in one of his earliest utterances he said that the purpose of Art, as of other rational activities, was to make men wiser and better.

Again, this passage from Mr. Stephen Reynolds's *A Poor Man's House* is worth a shelf of philosophic books on aesthetics:

'I am inclined to think that the taste of the poor, the un-educated, is on the right lines, though undeveloped, whilst the taste of the educated consists of beautifully developed wrong-ness, an exquisite secession from reality. . . . Degenerates love narcotics: their meats must be strange: they are afraid of the greatest things of life—the commonplace. Much culture has debilitated them. Rank life would kill them—or save them.'

It would be well for our own thinking if we returned to the older meaning given to 'aesthetic'. I find by accident in H. Morley's *English Writers* that the British schoolman Erigena made use, a thousand years ago, of the word *aesthesis* in the sense of perception, a feminine quality complementary to *nous*. In any case we need firm definitions of all these slippery words. Anything will do to think with if it is only made firm. 'Art', it seems to me, is right activity and work, especially complete and noble workmanship. Beauty in Art is the evidence of high humanity in work. Appreciation of Beauty should be one with our judgement of essential quality; there should be an instant recognition of what is noble and what is base. The sense of Beauty is the work-conscience.

It may be granted that colours, sounds, scents, and even

touch, will induce states of consciousness approximating to hypnosis and intoxication. If this field is specially marked off for aesthetics, well and good—or rather, well and bad; but the limitations should be very clearly stated, and it must be recognized that such forms of emotion are subject to diseases which are very dangerously infectious. Again, it should be foreseen that if the laws governing the production of free beauty could be discovered and written in a book, the possibility of its further existence in any high degree would thereby be abolished. No one could care for beauty produced by formulas. True revealing expression must always be unconscious. That which becomes known passes into the realm of science.

Whenever the tide turns towards a better and saner form of civilization, the preoccupation of philosophers with the narrow, vague, and betraying theories of aesthetics, as generally conceived, will make way for a philosophy of right labour. Education for enjoyment will be superseded by education for fine forms of production. Right doing and living will necessarily flow into noble types and beautiful forms. Here, too, those who work the will shall know the doctrine.

Chapter XV

Exhibitionism at the Royal Academy and Higher Criticism of Art [1]

I T used to be explained that the 'Higher Criticism' made no claim to the exaltation of status, but that it occupied other ground than the ordinary variety in trying to see particular facts in their wider relations. Such criticism, however it might be called, is required for all our modern institutions and professionalisms. It may hardly be realized by students of current thought, policies, and tendencies, how the annual show of pictures at the Royal Academy is arranged and catalogued matter for an estimate of the quality of modern existence. Those pictures, with the foreground of moving groups of 'sightseers', make a perfect cinematographic exhibition of well-to-do people and their desires. The paintings themselves by the economic 'higgling of the market', assisted by the skilled intervention of jurors and dealers, and the outflow of press comment, represent exactly what English culture expects of 'Art' in this year of grace—this special year following the war. There are here in fact many exhibitions—the waiting motors in the court, the great suite of galleries, the crowds flocking through the turnstiles to see the biggest

[1] *Hibbert Journal*, 1920.

picture-match of the year. The paintings themselves fur-
nish an absolutely perfect exhibition of exhibitionism.
There is much here to suggest thought, for if deep does
not call to deep, shallow reflecting shallow might evoke
another kind of profundity. Just this is what English
artists, trained, too, for the most part at the cost of the
State, have to supply to satisfy the national longing for
art. Observers and students require material, statistics, and
tabulated facts to work on. Here are all these excellently
arranged and indexed. What does it all mean from the
national, human, and—if I may use the word in my way
—from the religious point of view?

People have been put off by the propaganda that art is
a high mystery not to be understood by the uninitiated.
Why then do artists perform in public? There are, of
course, more technical and traditional approaches to art
valuation, but from the human point of view all that is
required is a clear shining mind to hold the mirror up to
fact. We need a study of the psychology of pictures which
shall recognize that in them we have minds invitingly laid
open before us. Painting is a language for mind and spirit
communication; well then, what does it say? These pictures make up indeed a composite photograph of the
British mind and heart in 1920—reverence, pity, love,
fashion, commercialism, low comedy and harlequinade
must be here in their due proportion, although I must confess I have thought that the latter categories are even over-
represented. The great picture-shows are only one class of
specimens of our ruling institutions at this time, and a
study of each of them should be put on record. In to-day's
paper I read, 'Miss Lena Ashwell, speaking at Cambridge

on Saturday, said that the artistic genius which ought to have been stirred by the war had no chance of finding expression because the entertainment of the people was in the hands of commercials. William Shakespeare would not have a dog's chance to-day.'

We are often told that art is imagination, and it may be admitted that imagination is one important factor. What imaginations have we at the Royal Academy? There is, in fact, hardly a design for a monumental, symbolizing, summarizing picture in the whole show. It is not that we have ceased to think in that way and cannot produce these imaginations, but it is a quite astonishing fact that such serious monumental designs of a national character have gravitated to *Punch*, where we accept them under the name of *cartoons*. The only serious designs that I have seen during and since the war which dared to touch the note of nobility have been in the comic press. Here the artist may still speak without the exhibition standard in his mind or the fear of dealers in his heart. Here we may still find the eye language of serious imaginations. In great epochs of civilization many of these comic-paper cartoons would have been thought worthy to be put into public frescoes and mosaics for speech with the people: now that paintings may only be seen behind barriers by paying gate-money, there is 'no demand for that sort of thing'. It is difficult to maintain an ideal in a deal!

We are also told that art requires an object seen through a temperament, and that it is the temperament that matters. Quite true in a way, so it is, and cannot be helped; in any case we are all 'temperaments'. We may take it for granted or go on to question the temperaments

and spirits what they be of. Should a painting temperament be balanced and central or, if not always that, should
it be eccentric in noble or ignoble ways?

Arguments have raged on the question how far 'subject' is of importance in painting, and an uncomfortable
feeling has been raised that to care for 'subject' or to have
an objection to vulgarity is vulgar. That is, it is suggested
that it is dull and bourgeois to care for touching and
teaching subject matters, but that the reverse and the
perverse do not count as such. There is here a dim reflection of a half-truth by accident. A gin bottle might, once
in a way, be painted more nobly than a lily; and always
it is not so much what the subject is *called* that matters as
the way it is 'seen'. It is a question of good-will, health,
and sanity; indeed, more and more we shall have to fight
to maintain sanity. I find a passage in a book by Michaelis,
the late great scholar of Greek art, which I must quote as
it shows how similar arguments on art for art's sake had
been 'made up' and pressed in Germany.

'The work of art has a language of its own, which it is
our task to understand and to explain. There is not only a
written but a pictorial tradition, each of which follows its
own laws. But it does not appear right to me—though these
may be unwelcome reflections—to appreciate in a work of art
only the form, in a picture the colour, and to declare the content more or less indifferent. Least of all can this be the case in
regard to ancient art. The painter Nikias observed that the
subject formed a part of painting. Ancient art knows as little
as ancient life of an absolute mastery of form. The Athenians
only considered the person perfect who combined beauty
with an inner efficiency, and ancient art is not different. It may

be conceded that Lysippos said the last word in perfecting Greek art, yet Phidias ranks above him, as his content is richer and higher, and his form equals his content. The form is only the robe which the content creates for itself. Content and form are inseparably one. It is only their relation to one another which determines the value of a work of art.'

Much well-intentioned talk about art is confusing because art is so many-sided, and while the speaker is thinking of *a* the listener hears in relation to *b*. Art is not only high imagination and invention, it is also skilled workmanship and patient record. It is 'design', but it is also imitation. All art is labour as well as thought. All *doing* indeed includes some *saying*, but some forms of art, like building, *do* more and *say* less; while other forms, as painting, while doing less should say far more. Their doing is for the saying's sake. Painting, indeed, is another form of language—thought addressed to the eye instead of to the ear. In all forms of art the spirit triumphs over mere brute toil. Art is best conceived as beneficent labour which blesses both him who gives and him who receives. Beauty is its evidence—Beauty is virtue in being.

The purpose of this little paper is to ask for interest in, and general understanding of, the functions of art by all who are interested in thought, and life, and civilization. I wish to suggest that the art of picture-painting must be studied from the human and communal points of view and not be left to breed in and in to the point of insanity.

One of the reasons for latter-day extreme doctrines and practice in painting is to be found in an attempt to find a ground not occupied by the photographic camera. Having made machines to draw, and paint, and sing, and act drama, we do not know what to do with ourselves. Art philosophies are very largely conditioned by economics; 'Cubism' and End-of-the-worldism are almost mechanically simple reactions from mechanism. If good art is a form of pleasant human speech, great art is teaching and worship. All art is the wisdom of men's hands. We cannot for long love triangles, zigzags, and jazzeries. Beauty is that which when seen we should love. I saw the other day that the elder Mr. Yeats had said that beauty is that which suggests affection—I quote from memory, but it seemed a critical saying which may hardly be bettered.

Of the current exhibition at the Royal Academy of Arts I will only venture to say that the four record pictures of the Peace Conferences seem to me to be far and away the most real and worth while. They at least have a reason for being, and they are wonderfully skilful. Then in order of reality come the portraits, and these too fill a want that seems to be felt. But—if I may say just what I think in a world where that is hardly permitted— the portraits as a whole, however clever they may be, seem to lack humanity. Many of them are like impersonations of success, competence, pride, force, riches, commercialism—masks rather than faces. Only one of those I saw seemed to be just a human creature: here there was tenderness, reflection, shyness—the mystery of a man; my heart leaped within me to see a soul. And this reminds me that English people as such have hardly been painted since Holbein; they have been painted as titles, or as property, or fox-hunting, or clothes and fashion. Reynolds was an exquisite painter of perukes, powder, and perfume; in his time, however, the position of a painter as another kind of valet was well understood. After the portraits come some decorative pieces, about half a dozen of which might be gay and delightful in a great financial dining-room or a restaurant. The next series in order of sincerity appeared to be the studies of 'interiors'; we are all interested in pleasant rooms and fine old furniture and tea-things. It is not exactly great-minded; but it is charming, so let us be thankful. As for the landscapes, there are several small portraits of places which are excellent and evidently done for love and interest. Of more grand-manner land-scape I do not remember any which had the moving quality, except perhaps one of Venice by a survivor from the last generation who holds something of Turner and Samuel Palmer by apostolic succession rather than by wilful revivalism. There seems indeed to be a noticeable failure in 'the will to' paint poetic landscape. It may be that men are unconsciously getting frightened by a feeling that untrampled country only remains in the narrow cracks between the railways and factories. To paint a landscape now requires so much 'leaving out' that hearts may well fail. As Morris said of one of Fred Walker's 'Idylls', 'But 'tisn't like that.' Up to now, indeed, our composed land-scapes have been canvas screens put up between us and our desecration of England.

Of course there are dozens of nice little pictures of slight incidents and pretty corners, very well done. As a whole, indeed, the artists are competent and sometimes amazingly skilful. It has been said recently that painters have lost the traditions of their art, but I have not found it explained whether this refers to the types of picture produced or to sound methods in workmanship. In the knowledge of pigments and how to mix and lay them so that pictures will last, there has probably been a most serious loss of workman-like tradition. ('You might make an artist, but a workman—never!' said Stevenson.) On the other hand, it must, in fairness, be said that the traditions which well-equipped modern painters still have are only acquired by earnest work for a dozen years. The loss of purpose and the general anarchy are largely the result of exhibitionism itself, by which our artificial standard takes the place of common realities. Still our painters and craftsmen of every kind would do true and impressive work if they could get out of the limelight of the Press and find other ways of employment than that of amusing the financial world. The great fact of the whole business is that we are witnessing the maturing of the Capitalistic school of painting. If the Royal Academy, as a powerful and wealthy corporation enjoying the hospitality of the nation in regard to its premises, had had guild rules, it might have been different, but possibly only in a small degree. The Royal Academy *régime*, as it is, has led to the sad identification of 'art' with painting, especially the oil variety, and further, with the sort of oil painting which is likely to sell at an annual bazaar and bring in gate-money. It is an old, and in many ways a generous body, but there is some danger of confusion between its functions as a semi-public institution and as a private corporation. While I am finishing this, I read: '*Purchase of Paintings.*—The President and Council of the Royal Academy have purchased the following works under the terms of the Chantrey Bequest: *Feeding the Fowls*, oil painting by ———, R.A.; *Epsom Downs*, oil painting by ———, A.R.A.' As far as may be judged from the titles, these do not appear to be pictures of an epic character and of national importance. The selection, however, is manifestly impartial as between the two classes of members of the institution.

Painting is properly a craft and should be organized as a trade-guild having relations with house-painting, the parent art. Then the drainage of all 'art' to London should be intercepted and diverted to many centres of civilization. Above all, public bodies should spend less in educating artists and more in obtaining sound work of all kinds in their several towns. It seems a silly sacrifice, this education for what is not required, or required only as oil paintings in gilt frames to hang on the walls of the smoking- and billiard-rooms of the 'moneyed classes'. They who pay for paintings certainly call the pictorial tunes. 'How can it be otherwise?' may be asked: but why should art students be brought up at the public expense for such a fate? Another way must be found at one end or the other. I said to a serious old student the other day that if the faculty for art was a 'gift', then its mission must be to *give* and not to show off. 'Yes', he replied, 'but no one wants our giving.'

Artists wish to give; they want to be allowed to work. A few 'fine arts', so called, are the last refuges left in a world which has destroyed reasonable employments. Artists have the proud distinction of making things, and doing something with their hands. Many, indeed most, of the rebellions in art and the resorts to shock tactics are the result of disillusion. The exhibitional way is too severe a task; a few only can fight their way through with expert swordsmanship to journalistic recognition and high prices. The heart of art must wither under such conditions. Art should be peaceable, modest, helpful, health-giving. 'All great art is praise'; yes! and—forgive the word for the meaning—the greatest pictures are preached. Was any sermon, indeed, of the whole nineteenth century so prophetic as Madox Brown's *Work*, with the philosophers and politicians of 1860 riding by on the other side for an outing? As it is, what has been accomplished save the stuffing of sale-rooms? Hardly anything has been done for a serious purpose since the Death of Nelson was painted at the Houses of Parliament. A private person may hardly be sure of getting a competent portrait painted without going to one of half a dozen fashionables and paying an unknown sum. We must begin again at the other end and commission young painters to do their best for ten or twenty pounds. That is on a small scale, and as drawings tinted or otherwise, rather than as show pieces in oil paint. The fact is, exhibitionist portraits do not make house portraits, nor gallery pictures room pictures, nor popular successes food for human joy. In truth there is an artificial standard all along 'the line'. Too many pictures are merely professional products. Picture-making may be strictly analogous to the better-understood 'book-making' exercise. The right way to get art is to pick a man and trust him to do something for you personally, if necessary mentioning a sum of money—'what can you do for me in painting up this room for fifty pounds?' That is the way our national arts might be improved. Visit local Art

Schools and draw out the spirit of locality. Every town should have its pleasantnesses (if any) and its antiquities (if not torn down) recorded, and its public buildings adorned in some civilizing way. The men are able and waiting, it is the tradition of employment which has broken down. We must bring back simplicity and confidence. The setting up of an aristocracy, an aesthetic house of lords, has not answered in the democracy of art. Was it this Blake had in mind when he said something to the effect that all are equal in the heaven of art? It is a great national question—the cause of art is the cause of civilization; but this exhibitionism is one of many symptoms of 'the sickness of acquisitive society'.

Chapter XVI

Ruskin: Defeat and Victory [1]

A N American journal recently printed an appreci-
ative centenary article entitled 'The Defeat of
Ruskin'. He, so it was said, had hoped that the
truth would make the people free; they, however, did not
wish to receive truth and freedom, and so his long strife
ended in defeat. But the end cannot be said to have come.
Perhaps, after all, so great is the coiled complexity of
human things, there may be no full and final defeat nor
yet victory. As time passes seeming opposites intermix and
weave the web of reality. On many fields, indeed, Ruskin
has already vanquished his conquerors as the mind of
Greece subjugated Rome.

A prophet, however much he may appear to be in
opposition to his age, yet in a peculiar way represents that
particular time. He is the antidote, the balance, the com-
plement, and his is the voice which awakes all those who
are ready to be like minded. If he is wholly successful, and
his teaching is absorbed, it may afterwards hardly be
understood how any one might ever have believed otherwise. The flashing inspiration becomes a commonplace. It
is the prophet's aim to be thus abolished in absorption; to
be lost by diffusion.

[1] Arts and Crafts Society, 1919.

Ruskin having been defeated while he lived has perhaps his greatest reward in being forgotten. His was not a business for showy recognition, but his thought saturates this generation through and through.

Arguments are endless, and criticism is vain unless it is convincing; as it is mostly practised it is merely recording how little men do not agree with big ones. The critic really is criticizing himself as those who judge are thereby judged. The writer of this little note would wish that some word might chance to explain Ruskin to any who think him difficult to understand. Like all men he was a compound. He was wistful and elf-like, just what we imagine of the Celtic temper; an artist and wit; something of an egoist driven by his loneliness, and yet the servant of all; a severe controversialist torn by compassion and compunction—a mixture of fury and tenderness. He was of like passions with ourselves, but as he said of Elijah, 'Yes, but he had them better under control', and ever his thoughts and efforts were set on building a reasonable society, a house for wisdom to dwell in. In all, his wit must be taken into consideration. When some one tried to convict him of inconsistency his reply was: 'No one should ever believe me until I have contradicted myself three times'! When another complained of his irony he replied that its only sting was in its truth.

Instead of turning over one of a score of volumes to find points to comment on I will quickly put down what I find in my mind as the general impression of his teaching:

1. Art is not a luxury, it is an essential element in all right work. 'Industry without art is brutality; life without

industry is guilt.' True work is the highest mode of life.

2. Science is not properly an endless heaping up of 'facts', regardless of form and direction; choice is involved; it should be wisdom and service.

3. Economics called political need not be identified with a theory of bank balances regardless of who holds the cheque books, and what the cheques are drawn for. A reasonable system of economics would be a doctrine of wise production and beneficent distribution. 'There is no wealth but life.' The 'orthodox' economists who had forgotten life, who never heard of quality in workmanship, and neglected even to foresee war, nearly burst themselves with rage at such simple utterances.

4. Education need not necessarily be conceived as an introduction to the competitive scramble, it might be a tempering of the human spirit.

5. An artist, poet, or musician is not properly an acrobat engaged in showing off, his proper office is to teach and inspire.

6. The land is not a mine for exploitation and a dumping heap for refuse, but it is our garden home.

7. Property must observe propriety.

8. Quality of life is the end of all rational activity.

It was a thousand pities that Ruskin wrote some petulant words about Whistler's exquisite '*Nocturne*', but if we approach this unfortunate matter from the side of Ruskin's 'principles' and 'doctrine', we may get to understand even that; it was like Morris's disregard of the magnificence of St. Paul's, and Tolstoy's doubt as to what he would have to do if his grandmother were being attacked. It was the logic of a position.

Once I had the delight of hearing the master—it was at one of the 'Storm Cloud' series. Here, in a lecture as it was given, more than half asides, he explained how he had studied sunsets and cloud formation, 'bottling records as my father bottled wine'. One observation he told us of was of a cloud effect seen at Coniston. In crystal clear air a pure white cloud had a patch of iridescence 'like—like —why like a handful of jewels thrown on a snow bank'.[1]

[1] In the late exhibition of his drawings I recognized one as being of this phenomenon.

Chapter XVII

Political Economy or Productive Economy [1]

M Y little paper has not written itself with the tone I like, but this, I hope, is only the result of compression. When I promised to write a note on the Arts and Crafts and Political Economy, I hardly sufficiently felt the rashness of using the words 'Political Economy' without being an expert in the 'orthodox' writings. In fact, when one thinks of it, it is bold for the ordinary person to use nearly any words or to have any opinions on any subject whatever. As things go on, they become more complex and can only be dealt with by specialization, so that no place is left for the average man of goodwill. It seems that the chaos of warring philosophies should be settled as a preliminary, then the inquirer would find other 'subjects' like Ethics and Psychology, which properly should be dealt with before he came to the hundred volumes on Economics—all dismal. Even then he must not teach till he has taken a certificate in pedagogy. If, as a matter of fact, a mere man ventures to touch on any subject whatever without some such preparation, he is at the mercy of the trained assassin's polished weapons of debate. Fancy venturing a word on

[1] Arts and Crafts Society, 1915.

theology to an Archbishop! It is like that to speak of Political Economy with the humblest of its professors. It may not be done: he turns with hurt surprise and then says drily (as Tolstoy noticed) 'Ah, but have you read Schwartzberg?' The priests of Economics seem to shield their doctrines with a theory of inspiration. Everything depends on it, the priest of Economics will tell you, but unless you are initiated you can't understand; 'you must' (and here the fanatic blazes out) 'receive it as written, it is political economy and settled'! But this is only their way with the outer world: amongst themselves, their science, so called, is rent through and through and across like a torn-up letter, and their quarrels are so bitter that they have (happy paradox) to take the plain man into their confidence to arbitrate between them. I am now arbitrating.

For the purpose of this paper, I thought I should best obtain a neutral statement as to what it was all about, and what it proposed to do, in the new *Encyclopaedia Britannica*, and here, as a matter of fact, I found that doubt, disillusion, and disintegration had gone farther than I had any suspicion of. The article is half apology, half an alarm. There are only three or four positive statements in the whole thing, and these are qualified in effect to this— Political Economy concerns itself with wealth (if any one could say what should be considered wealth): a sound system would be of great value in international relations (if such a system could be found): a statistical method of inquiry is probably the best (if one could know what to inquire about and could get hold of all the factors of the problem, which in itself is almost impossible). After more

hedging and some mystification, the most positive statement in this scientific article is reached, and that is a piece
of commonplace rhetoric:—

'At present, ethics has more to learn from economics than
the latter has from ethics.'

Then come the outpourings of confidence, of which I
copy a sentence or two:

(1) 'The economists of the classical period, with the one
exception of Adam Smith, will be forgotten, and the *Wealth
of Nations* itself has long ceased to be a scientific text-book.
The "old Political Economy" is not likely (in the future) to be a
question of any interest.'

(2) 'In fact, there never was a scientific system at all; what
was mistaken for it was fashioned by men whose interests were
practical rather than scientific, who could not write correct
English and revealed in reasoning the usual fallacies. . . . So
the "old Political Economy" lies shattered.'

(3) There is (at present) 'economic agnosticism, combined
with unwillingness to cut adrift from old moorings'.

This is all rather astonishing from the expert of the
Encyclopaedia. In aiming his bolts at the heads of other
economists and leading up to his conclusion, which is
'see, Chamberlain, Joseph', he seems to have forgotten
that non-professors will read the mixture of assertion and
avowal which gives the whole 'science' away.

There is little, hardly a word, about building up a
strong and healthy state, nothing of beautiful and learned
cities, nothing of sound work and fair art, nothing of a
noble and confident national spirit: little beyond text-book
exposition and despair. The writer does not even say

whether that which ethics is to take from economics is the celebrated axiom that men's actions are founded in self-interest.

The truth is, as anybody who just knows the lie of the land will see at once, there are an infinite series of possible political economies. The system of Judea was one, the system of Athens was another, and that of Sparta a third. In our own day, the Germans, I believe, sweep aside English political economy as mere 'Manchesterdom'. There can be no one scheme of economics which shall apply to peoples in varying stages of development. What we require is a scheme of national economy which shall be ideal or serviceable to us.

Our problem like that of Judea, of Athens, of Sparta, is to dare to think a theory of the State, then to educate a national spirit which shall sustain it, and further to draw our economics and sciences into helpful and harmonious relations with it. We have to bring all our arts, sciences, and philosophies to the service of life in the State, for without such a centre they run to waste in the infinite sands.

This political economy was never broad-based on general considerations of national welfare: it has always been the apologetic of commercial expansion and, in its attempt to make itself look like a science, it has taken up the position of analysing what comes of verbal definitions rather than of pointing to an ideal. In the language of the moment, it is a 'cross-section', not a stream, it is static not moving. On its own ground and at play with its own definitions, its reasoning may sometimes have been fairly correct in form, but the ground was not that of the real world, and as a science it may be compared to pre-Copernican astronomy—it had no centre to its system. We seek in vain in it for guidance in regard to such serious questions as national vitality, intelligence, and spirit. There is no sufficient discrimination as to what are desirable employments, and it does not make plain that the quality of the people can only be kept up by the practice of highly skilled industries. There is too much about bulk, too little about quality. There is no appreciation of the meaning of Art, and generally no teaching on the needs for good life in our towns, which may be hideous and wretched for all the political economist seems to care. He does not sufficiently point out that the energy of a nation should be given rather to production than to dealing. It is not merely a question of profit, but too much dealing seems to kill production and high intelligence.

Like our other philosophers, the economists have wanted to find out some isolated 'truth', some new philosopher's stone. They have not seen political theory as part of the problem of action. They never, for instance, thought of such questions as—What would happen if, under machine rule, men forgot the crafts of their hands? If most of the art interest of the country for fifty years is directed by dealers to antiques, what will happen to productive art? Does it pay best for towns to be fair or foul? Suppose millions are put into 'art' education, and nobody will have any art when it is educated, of what good is the education? What are the relative advantages of a production for quality as against quantity production? Is it desirable, all things considered, including our relations with India, that the use of true Indigo dyes should be abandoned? Compare the vague abstractions of any of our economical writers with the masterly memorandum of Hakluyt (in 1582):

'touching natural vent of our commodities and the labour of our poor people withall and of the general enriching of the realm . . . and to bring in the excellence of the art of Dyeing . . . to endeavour the sale of such of our cloths as be coloured with our own natural colours rather than with foreign colours. But with this proviso always, that our cloth goes out with as much labour of our people as may be: for it would be madness to vent our wool not in cloth. . . . Also, not to carry out any cloth white, but dyed, if it may be, that the subjects of this realm may take as much benefit as possible.'

Then, for proper groundwork and motive, take the statement—

'Men are born as well to seek the common commodity of their country as their own private benefit.'

That is politics and economics and sociology and common sense. How clearly is here understood the immense importance of keeping alive the skilled crafts, as against falling back on crude labour and the selling of England itself in the form of coal and iron. Without art and culture ideals, it is evident that the productivity of a state is always tending to lower levels. If we do not weave and dye, we have to hew coal and smelt iron. We have to try to get the value of national arts and crafts understood by the vague and visionary writers on economics who love to deal with it all in mass by mathematical formulas, ignoring all questions of quality as disturbing elements, and chattering about 'unskilled labour'—little they know!

It is only two years since that the economically wise

were very anxious as to whether it would be right to take
due measures to bring back the art of dyeing, but they
seem to have been won over by calling it a 'key
industry'—great in 'science' is the power of words—
should we laugh or cry? Now, however, that the new
catchword has been invented, we must try to get what we
can out of it. For instance, if we keep on saying that
Spitalfields silk-weaving is a 'key industry', it is possible
we might get the real economists to give it a thought
before it is too late.

A reasonable system of productive economy would not
begin in mid-air with expositions that capital is a wages
fund, and so on, but it would lay out a scheme on visible
foundations, such as—

1. Work and Food.
2. Clothing and Health.
3. Shelter and Family Life.
4. Community and Justice.
5. Motives and Sanctions.
6. Ends of Production, &c., &c.

I have left little time to speak of the arts in relation to
economics, but I do want to say that here again our
besetting trick of seeking water-tight isolation has done
us terrible harm, and we have isolated our art until most
people seem to think in the equation: Art = Oil-paintings
by a real R.A. They do not realize that the next stage will
be that that is not art either; it will wither for want of roots.

Art is the element of good quality in all production,
and perhaps the greatest problem of all just now is this one
of art. Certainly, to a commercial nation, the need to keep
up the quality of its goods is vital. It is essential to national

persistence that skilled industries should be maintained as against falling back on unskilled ones; for the craft subdues the craftsman to that he works in. If we are driven from the traditional crafts into mere crude labour, we have become an enslaved nation. I have lately seen this truth very clearly set out in the publications of the German *Werkbund*. Industry requiring intelligence must be maintained by Germans, because intelligence is necessary to them as a nation, and some residuum of interest in work helps to content the worker.—Think of that now! Soon after the Franco-German war, a consciously thought-out effort was begun to capture for Germany all scientific and skilled crafts—they might be useful in time of war, for one thing. Nearly twenty-five years ago, I was in a railway carriage in East Europe, somewhere near Nisch, I fancy, when a German commercial traveller, knowing all languages and possessing competitive enthusiasm, pulled a nice four-bladed knife out of his pocket. 'That's as good as Sheffield, isn't it?' said he. About six years ago, it was decided in Germany to adapt the English Arts and Crafts to their machine industries, and so the *Werkbund* [1] just mentioned was formed, which in marvellously quick time has brought a commercially captivating type of design into vogue. Personally, I hate it, but it was not done for me.

Germany proposes that *we* shall not do any dyeing of stuffs, or clock-making, or instrument-making, or piano-making, or even any wall-paper printing. Coal-digging is quite good enough for us, and I suppose, if the aggregate

[1] Naumann and others of the ablest modern economists in Germany are, I believe, interested in the ideals of the *Werkbund*.

trade returns are kept up for owners and shippers, the economists won't much mind; nor will they foresee coal difficulties before they come. As the *Encyclopaedia* said, they don't like to relinquish their 'old moorings'.

Only six months or so before the war, quite a learned Austrian came to call on me. He had taken his Doctor's degree in Political Economy, and he told me his thesis was on—what do you think?—'The Arts and Crafts', which now form, he said, a well-defined branch of political science in Germany. He hoped to get appointed to a chair in this particular department. No English economist has ever heard of the Arts and Crafts, I fear; certainly none would waste his time in calling on me. Our economist is probably engaged on some abstract theory in 'pure' economics on 'coefficients of value', without having any more idea about the value of design than a cat. My Austrian said he had come to England as the Mother-land of the Arts and Crafts, but he was disappointed with what he had seen; the untidy streets, miserable railway stations, inefficient architecture, were entirely different from what he had been led to expect from the fame of the Arts and Crafts which he had come to inspect. In a frank way, he was almost scornful. 'How is it,' he said, 'that you, who had it all twenty years ago, are now neglecting the Arts and Crafts?' I did not like to explain to him that our press was very interested in exhibitions of oil-paintings and dealing in antiques, and that, moreover, there was the sportsman's love of killing things, so that the critics (so called) after a year or two of doubting indulgence to a new plaything, had practically killed our craft exhibitions: moreover, in this country, art was settled by the R.A.

I remember that I asked this Austrian Doctor of Arts and Crafts why it was that no such branch of the 'science of wealth' as his was recognized here, and why we had no professorships like his, say in Liverpool or London, not Oxford, of course. 'I do not know,' he said, 'but the competition, *it* will make you.' My heart sank within me: here was a man of academic distinction, but without 'side', who not only talked to me mind to mind, but who also looked at things with his eyes, instead of for ever spinning word arguments in the void.

If we art workers could combine in some way with the people calling themselves scientific economists, some good might come out of it. We know hard facts about quality in workmanship, the limit of untidiness in cities and the advertisement disease, which no people calling itself civilized should endure. We know about the crafts and design and architecture and outward order in the cities of Europe. We have eyes. On their side, they have unction and conviction; they can touch the springs of faith in the modern mind about 'science' with texts on supply and demand, margins of economic rent, and laws of diminishing returns. As it is, those who produce, and have eyes that see, are everywhere enslaved by busy people with office-boy wits. That I take it is the true, scientific, and economic reason for the clear failure to produce genius, beauty, or happiness. With the Arts and Crafts lies the founding of a new school of Productive Economy in England.

.   .   .   .   .

'To centralize wealth is to disperse the people: to distribute wealth is to collect the people.' (Chinese maxim.)

Chapter XVIII

Arts and the Function of Guilds [1]

MANY ideas are usually covered by the little word
Art. Ordinary manipulative skill and the greatest
imaginative design are both Art. Now, in one
sense, Art is merely a matter of routine training. With
industry, any one can learn to draw, any one can learn to
paint, any one can learn sculpture. That is, 'more or less'
of course; but still, given sufficient application, a large
proportion of persons could be taught to practise any
of these arts with considerable skill. We need clearly
to realize that such painting, sculpture, and ornamentation are entirely unnecessary things, and, produced for a
thoughtless market, they may be worse than useless. It is
desirable to gain clear sight of the distinction between this
ordinary commercial output called art and really fresh and
vital work. There is nothing especially honourable in
doing so many commonplace pictures or sculptures to be
exhibited in galleries because it passes under the name of
Art.

In the higher arts, some very distinct gift is required;
it may be supreme skill in handling, with only average
power of thought, but more generally it will be the power

[1] *The Quest* (Birmingham), 1896.

of suggesting ideas and stimulating the imagination. Without these, the higher arts fail of their chief reason for existence. The mere manufacture of so many thousands of pictures and statues, of so many yards of ornamentation and tons of illustrated journals, may well become a burden to society. For such reasons as these, I think that the way leading to the practice of 'unapplied' art should be thickly set with notice-boards and man-traps. Only a genius should be permitted to follow 'fine art' exclusively.

On a different plane to that of the imaginative arts of design rest the illustrative arts, and here there is room for less than genius. It is a great pity that careful natural history drawing is so little in favour, and that the art of copying pictures is not encouraged. One careful drawing from nature, or one good copy of a fine picture, is worth a dining-room full of middling paintings. Every school-room in the country might have a Giotto and a Turner which only an expert could distinguish from originals, if supply and demand might be arranged to work to such an end. Old architecture should be drawn before 'restoration' has too far falsified every building in the country. Such records will, at a day not far distant, be almost the only memorials of our ancient national architecture.

But the safest, widest standing-ground for most of us is to deal with art only in relation to the making of necessary things—to deal with it as craftsmen. This brings before us the great problems of modern days: How can ordinary wares once more be made beautiful? How can the modern city be made less hideous? It is not by endeavouring to

M

produce a few geniuses that general production will be much bettered: beauty can only be brought back to common life by our doing common work in an interesting way. We seem for the most part to think that the way in which we see work carried on day by day is very much in the nature of things, that 'it always has been so and always will be so'. The study of the past, however, shows us that, so far from its always having been so, production has recently become art-less for the first time in history. Some knowledge of the crafts, particularly those of Greece and the Middle Ages, enables us to interpret history in a way unknown to students of books alone.[1] By comparing the works then produced with other records, it becomes abundantly evident that the most distinctive characteristic of the Middle Ages was the honourable position in the State then taken up by labour.

In every city which did anything, from Florence and Nuremburg to Paris and London, the craftsmen were not only honoured citizens but, through the organized craft guilds, masons, bakers, tanners, largely governed the towns. I do not mean tradesmen 'retired' and respectable, but workers with their aprons on. How about the Feudal Lords? At bottom, aristocracy rests on the conquest of one body of people by another, usually of different race. In one sense the nobles of the Middle Ages formed a class almost as much apart as if they had possessed wings. Still, they were but a section of society, not a stratum over the whole area: as has been well said, society was then divided vertically, not horizontally. The nobles formed, as it were, the guild of war lords, as the Church formed the guild for

[1] Cf. Prof. Petrie as quoted facing the title-page.

religion; but labour also won an estate in the towns and governed them openly. The town of the Middle Ages was an assemblage of craftsmen and traders governed by the delegates of their organizations. The King knocked at Temple Bar, to be admitted by the goldsmith or mercer who, as mayor, represented the citizens.

Step by step with the assumption of power by the craft guilds in the Free Towns, architecture—that is, the harmonious association of all the crafts—progressed, until the towns of Europe were not mere squalid heaps of bricks and mortar, but great organic works of art.

The bettering of the conditions of labour, in respect to shortening hours of work and increasing wages as much as may be, is not a very large or philosophic programme for the immense organization of the modern trade unions. Is that to be their only purpose, and are their functions to cease when that is worked out? I hope not; the crafts are theirs, and they must see to all that concerns them. Why should not the unions have apprentices enter into agreements with them, as apprenticeship to employers has almost entirely broken down? The unions should also see to it that wares are of a certain standard quality. They have, in a word, to find a way in which beautiful craftsmanship will once again become so common that it will reach the homes of their members.

We are now so unaccustomed to beauty that we are apt to look upon it as luxury and to regard with suspicion those who talk of art: and, indeed, I began by admitting that much which passes by the name is sheer waste and foolishness. But the art with which we are here concerned is nothing more than an intelligent mastery in work done;

it is the element of quality in workmanship. Unfortunately, as quality cannot easily be measured by statistics, that self-deluded person, the economist, has proceeded to ignore it altogether, and has dealt with labour only as quantity. Quality in workmanship has been very largely destroyed in the name of science and wealth. I can see no hope of labour being de-brutalized by the isolated works of the self-regarding art-genius or by the efforts of the ignorant political expert; organized labour can alone accomplish it.

Whatever the trade societies do or leave undone, they must ultimately, if they are to continue, take up the supervision of quality in the common interest. If society generally gets to understand that the unions, as far as may be, are interesting themselves in the quality of commodities, it will soon pay back the debt in sympathy. The unions, in a word, must become craft guilds, and, as such, be responsible to society in their several mysteries: they must discuss materials and methods and build up a new tradition of worthy workmanship. Only the properly proficient must become master-craftsmen: foremen in the guilds must be the only foremen acceptable in the works. The architect must be the man who has gone through the shops and the masons' or carpenters' guild, and is elected 'Master' by the suffrage of those who know what good workmanship is. I don't mean elected to any particular work, of course: the employer comes in there: but passed on as a qualified master under whom members of the guild will serve. If the existing middleman-contractor won't permit good work, he must be set aside. If the existing architect will not join in the quest for beauty, which is delightful craftsmanship, he too must go. These must both learn that theirs are not vested interests against society, but that they are the servants of society.

Chapter XIX

Art and Workmanship [1]

WE have been in the habit of writing so lyrically of art and of the temperament of the artist that the average man who lives in the street, sometimes a very mean street, is likely to think of it as remote and luxurious, not 'for the likes of him'. There is the danger in habitual excess of language that the plain man is likely to be frightened by it and it may be feared that much current exposition of the place and purpose of art only widens the gap between it and common lives.

A proper function of criticism should be to foster our national arts and not to frighten timid people off with high-pitched definitions and far-fetched metaphors mixed with a flood of (as Morris said) 'sham technical twaddle'. It is a pity to make a mystery of what should most easily be understood. There is nothing occult about the thought that all things may be made well or made ill. A work of art is first of all a well-made thing. It may be a well-made statue or a well-made chair, or a well-made book. Art is not a special sauce applied to ordinary cooking; it is the cooking itself if it is good. Most simply and generally art may be thought of as *the well-doing of what needs doing*. If

[1] *The Imprint*, 1913.

the thing is not worth doing it can hardly be a work of art, however well it may be done. A thing worth doing which is ill done is hardly a thing at all.

Fortunately people are artists who know it not—boot-makers (the few left), gardeners and basket-makers, and all players of games. We do not allow shoddy in cricket or football, but reserve it for serious things like houses and books, furniture and funerals.

If it is necessary that everything must be translated into words, our art critics might occupy quite a useful place if they would be good enough to realize that behind the picture-shows of the moment is the vast and important art of the country, the arts of the builder, furniture maker, printer, and the rest, which are matters of national well-being.

It is doubtful if we have it in us to form a leading school of painting at the present time; indeed, we seem to be occupied in trying to catch up with Europe at the wrong moment. It cannot be doubted, however, that we might lead in the domestic arts. And this is shown by the great interest which foreign observers take in the English Arts and Crafts movement. The Germans, indeed, who know the history of this development in England better than we do ourselves, realizing its importance from an economic point of view, have gone so far as to constitute a special branch of political economy which shall deal with the subject. One university, I believe, has established a professor's chair in the economics of arts and crafts. English study of fine lettering has in Germany been put into types which English printers are hastening to buy. We have now many highly trained men among us who might make books as notable as those of the finest presses if there were a steady demand for fine modern work.

During the last thirty years many English designers have set themselves to learn the crafts as artists; that is, so that they may have complete mastery of both design and workmanship. I may remark here that a characteristic of a work of art is that the design interpenetrates workmanship as in a painting, so that one may hardly know where one ends and the other begins. The master-workman, further, must have complete control from first to last to shape and finish as he will. If I were asked for some simple test by which we might hope to know a work of art when we saw one I should suggest something like this: *Every work of art shows that it was made by a human being for a human being.* Art is the humanity put into workmanship, the rest is slavery. The difference between a man-made work and a commercially-made work is like the difference between a gem and paste. We may not be able to tell the difference at first, but, when we find out, the intrinsic worth of the one is self-evident. Still it is highly important that commercial work shall be properly done after its own kind.

Although a machine-made thing can never be a work of art in the proper sense, there is no reason why it should not be good in a secondary order—shapely, smooth, strong, well fitting, useful; in fact, like a machine itself. Machinework should show quite frankly that it is the child of the machine; it is the pretence and subterfuge of most machine-made things which make them disgusting.

In the reaction from the dull monotony of early Victorian days it must be admitted that many workers fell into the affection of over-designing their things. Rightly understood, 'design' is not an agony of contortion but an effort to arrive at what will be obviously fit and true. The best design is one which, cost apart, should become a commonplace. A fine piece of furniture or a fine bookbinding should be shaped as inevitably as a fiddle.

Usually the best method of designing has been to improve on an existing model by bettering it a point at a time; a perfect table or chair or book has to be very well bred.

Another phase of the reaction from modern ways has been an excessive regard for old things, so that original workers have not had a fair chance of maintaining the full traditions of their arts. For instance, the social results of 'collecting old furniture' of course were not foreseen, but they certainly inflicted great injury on an essentially noble craft. At the present moment people who would like to do things in the best way would be well advised to have what they require made by capable men in modern forms. Now that we know all about it there is something pawnshoppy about gatherings from auctions, and the highly misdirected skill of the imitator has often made it next to impossible for even the expert to tell the difference between an original work and a copy.

Of course the scarcity, value, and historical interest of old pictures, and of books printed by Caxton, made it inevitable that they should be sought for and bought at great prices, but undoubtedly such collecting of antiques has had a most injurious effect on all kinds of modern production. One of the great phenomena of recent time has been a drift away from production towards dealing. We have to re-establish doing.

Of many problems this one of bringing back art to workmanship is not the least serious, or the most hopeful. It is a tremendous thing that whereas a century or so ago the great mass of the people exercised arts, such as bootmaking, bookbinding, chair-making, smithing, and the rest, now a great wedge has been driven in between the craftsman of every kind and his customers by the method of large production by machinery. 'We cannot go back'—true; and it is as true that we cannot stay where we are.

Once more let me try to make it clear that by art, instructed thinkers do not only mean pictures or quaint and curious things, or necessarily costly ones, certainly not luxurious ones. They mean worthy and complete workmanship by competent workmen.

ART IS THOUGHTFUL WORKMANSHIP.

Chapter XX

The Foundation in Labour [1]

B Y way of text to my little sermon, the words occur to me: 'Let him labour with his hands.' By way of illustration to my subject, the following little story was told me only an hour ago from some lives of early Breton saints. A monk of, say, the sixth century, having laboured in the fields all day, found that a little bird had built its nest in the mantle he had laid on the ground. Understanding what labour meant, he lent his cloak to the bird for the rest of the season.

I was asked to lecture on Art in the life of the worker, but I begged to be allowed to change the title into *Work and the Worker*. I find the word Art is a very ambiguous one which wants yards of definition before one can venture to say anything clear about it; and, for myself, I have long settled that what I elected to call Art was not some high essence which might lead to aesthetic excitements, but simply any sound and complete form of human work: the art of agriculture, the art of cookery, the art of picture painting, and so on. Human work, I say, not machine grinding. Machining is no more real work than hand-organ noises are real music.

[1] *The Highway,* 1917.

As societies and men come of age in the several ages of the world they awake to the consciousness that they make use of words and that little but custom settles the meaning of those words. Justice, art, morality, what do they mean? Then custom itself begins to break up and a new problem arises. The question is not now, What do the words actually mean? but: As we have these nice words in use, what meaning shall we fit to them? 'Philosophy, religion, liberty, the State', what shall we make these old words mean? This was the problem of Plato; this is the problem of to-day. Now we find ourselves in the possession of the little word Art, about which such heaps of rubbish have been written and in the name of which so many sillinesses are committed. What shall we make it mean?

Philosophers have noticed that certain forms of production tend to be free from direct material service and to become media for expressing emotion directed to the end of giving delight, or stimulus, to others. Modern use is in favour of trying to limit the use of the word Art to this aesthetic essence or its manifestation. Now this would be all right if it were not all wrong, wrong in history and wrong in results. Historically, the word Art has meant work, production, making, doing, and it was not conceived that the spirit, the expression, the meaning of the several kinds of work could be separated from a residuum which without it becomes brute labour. Art is the *substance* as well as the *expression*; it is the *service* as well as the *delight*; and the two aspects cannot be torn apart except to the ruin of both.

Thus the art of speech may be conceived as oratory,

eloquence, or rhetoric, but these things are only dangerous diseases without the serious meaning and purpose. There is an attractive aesthetic of the cooking art, but it is dangerous if too much thought is given to its thrills. Art, the aesthetic ones say, is intuition, imagination, pure lyricism, and so on and on. Very true in a way, but very dangerous. It is only true, indeed, when you say nothing about it. Tell a child that his manners and ways and tricks are wonderful art, and if you can get him to understand you have frozen the free beauty (which was inherent in healthy action) into affectation and etiquette. Our concern is with the veracities of conduct, speech, work; the expression, the beauty, the emotion will take care of themselves. Do I make myself clear? I do not deny the poetical content of workmanship, but what I do say is: Keep the work, the service, the meaning, strong and healthy, and due expression is bound to be there, too. In concentrating too much on the emotional content in certain chosen forms, as poetry, music, painting, you are, firstly, beating down other forms of production into non-arts, into mere brute labour; and, secondly, by isolating those very selected arts themselves too much from service and the common understanding you lay them open to speedy disease and decay. Beauty is the flowering of labour and service.

Art, then, I choose to believe, is sound and complete human workmanship. A work of art is a well-made boot, a well-made chair, a well-made picture.

The purpose of this little lecture is to say that to me work is not only art, but it is almost everything else as well. The 'Curse' if you will, but also the blessing, the discipline, the subject-matter of life. Work is a great Necessity, one of the absolute things. We have to learn to accept, and even to worship, work. We live by consumption, consumption of fuel, food, clothing, service. Is it not strange that this should be obviously so and yet that there is no body of teaching as to this great prime essential of life? I remember only a few years ago reading the pronouncement of some sweet and cultivated soul as to the ideal man. The ideal man, he thought, should be a Christian, a gentleman, a scholar, and an athlete, and I almost think he had to have a sense of humour as well. Very nice, though, perhaps, a little cloistered; but really not thick enough for life. We must gather together a teaching about life which recognizes that life is founded on work. We have to induce a deep reverence for work and the worker. Work is paying one's way; it is service; it is honour and righteousness. There may have been other words for other times, but for us the password is *Work*. In the last few generations—there are fashions in these things—there has been much talk of self-sacrifice, very confusing, as I can testify, to growing youths; but there has been far too little telling about service, service of cleaning drains, ploughing, and building. Why is it so? Why is the great continuous and necessary martyrdom of hard labour so universally and constantly ignored?

There have been deep historical causes which have led philosophers and teachers of all kinds to ignore the basis of life in work and to begin their thinking high in the air. For one thing, the problems, or, at least, the kind of problems which philosophers have ever since gone turning round and round, were set by the Greeks, and notably by Plato. Now the Greek State was founded on slavery, and it simply did not do for the boldest thinkers to question that. Labour was provided by the very constitution of things, and the great talking men worried little more about it than we do about the philosophies of horses and cows. After correcting their slaves in the morning they would put on the philosopher's garb, meet in the portico, and discourse exquisitely on the nature of justice and the essence of aesthetic delight.

At what we call the revival of learning, we took over all this body of thought and called it specifically philosophy, not recognizing that it was in no sense a complete scheme of thinking for life (for you cannot live on theories as to how you really know knowledge, but have to have bread and boots as a preliminary). Philosophy thus became the thinking of those with nothing else to do.

Then at the end of the classical period another way of thinking arose which involved in some degree a philosophy of labour. It seems to have been obscured and overlaid, but still there it is, and an objecting modern thinker has called it slave morality. How far it was complete I will not venture to say, but, looking at it historically, it may not be denied that Christianity did include within itself a body of teaching in regard to the slave, the labourer, the poor. It was, to some degree at least, the scheme of thinking of working men.

Turning from this backward view, it seems to me that in all the weltering, infinite field of thought-possibilities we just at this time can only hope to find a firm constructive centre in the idea of a noble, just, and inclusive civilization. A civilization inspired by a teaching which shall not ignore the groundwork, the first needs of life, but which shall be based here and now on common labour, a common life, and a common aim.

I do not say this as an idealist and would-be philanthropist, but as one who wants a more reasonable and beautiful world for himself. As it is, one cannot sufficiently hide away from the ugliness of things under about £4,000 a year, a country house, and two motors.

The question of machinery is one that troubles many minds, as well it may. At times I am drawn to the belief that machinery, gunpowder, electricity are too astounding powers for feeble-willed men to control. Indeed, it is quite thinkable that machinery is the wrecking force in the world, which will, in fact, be shattered by it. But, some will say, 'Machinery has come to stay.' That may be true. Drunkenness seems to have come to stay, but we have at least to try to *control* it. Machine production has, in fact, swiftly changed the character of our population, and whereas, not many generations ago, they were mostly craftsmen—that is, little artists—they are now an aggregate of machine-tenders, under gangers. These are the sort of facts which political economists never foresaw. Machinery is such a mighty power that it must be controlled; and I must say that mass production by machinery should imply production for the mass. No single individual should fire off a powerful machine for his own profit any more than he should work a cannon in Oxford Street to the terror of well-doers. The owner of machinery must be licensed to shoot. In truth, machinery is the artillery of commerce, and it must be controlled by wise generalship. We have as much right to control any form of machinery as we have to protect ourselves from firearms.

At the same time, all our ideals are so complicated by the huge question of international commerce that our very survival through this machine age may depend on our working the cranks and wheels as well as others. The position may be likened to that of a coach plunging down-hill after a team of maddened horses. It is not the time for any horse or the driver to give way to his private wishes to lie down; the facts of the position may best be dealt with by racing along. Nevertheless, machinery must be controlled; it must not be allowed, for instance, to go on ruining our towns and country-side so much as in the immediate past. Machinery must be controlled.

I shall be told that I have ignored brainwork; so in a way I have, as I have ignored amusement work. Much of this talk of brainwork is a trick parallel to the dividing off of art from labour. Do you not think that the skipper of the fishing-boat or the thatcher of the cornrick works with his brain as usefully as a company promoter or member of Parliament? Why, of course he does. But we do want brainwork in the modern sense, the very best that may be got, and it is worth paying extortionate charges, as we do to good doctors, if we cannot get it otherwise. But it needs to be good brainwork used in the interest of civilization and not forming a camp against it. How might we hope to secure that?

N

We have to set up a sympathetic and understanding contact and contract between all brain-workers and the completer men who work both with hands and brain. How may our brain-workers, directors, and teachers obtain such a contact with labour? First, some teaching about the service of labour must be got into all our educational schemes, not only in the elementary schools— the children there are likely to learn in another way later —but at Eton, Oxford, and theological seminaries. It must be impressed in our very natures as one of the *great things* of life.

There are many, especially old-fashioned, people who in their families have had close touch with poverty, who have a horror, deeply inlaid in their hearts, of waste of food. The new automobile way of thinking, 'I can pay for it, and do what I like with my own', does not appeal to them; they have a superstition in their very bones that waste of food is what used to be called wicked. Many, I am sure, feel a similar reverence for labour and the results of labour. Waste of food is waste of a means of life; but waste of labour is the waste of life itself, it is half murder, it has something of the horribly and blackly satanic about it. To my mind, it is the great typical modern sin. It had hardly arisen when the Decalogue was written.

This is the point above all others that I have tried to say which I should like to din and dint into your minds by repetition. We have drifted into easy ways of life and live behind screens, really not knowing what the world of winning the bare means of life is like. Money is a key which we apply, and the results of labour just flow from a tap if you have the key. *You get it at shops.*

Consumption, we have even been told, is good for trade. If a better type of civilization is ever to be developed, one of the very corners of the scheme must be understanding of and reverence for labour. Reverence for labour is the basis of art, for art is the labour which is fully worthy of reverence.

But merely being told is not enough. If ever we are to have a reasonable apprenticeship to life, say, in 500 years time, it will have to include some actual service in labour. This is not a joke, but a true ideal which I should like for myself and everybody. We all, as part of a normal minimum training in manliness, should be apprenticed to State service for at least a year. No one should be allowed to pass into 'brain-work' such as stockbroking without his year of manual drill; and others—Members of Parliament, architects, and all kinds of pastors and teachers—should, I think, be asked to have two years to show their good faith. If there were this basis of actual experience, then, perhaps, we might hope to control the machines before they tear civilization to bits.

Again, and I suggest this as an immediate policy, some acknowledged turnpike should be made by which a certain percentage of those in our schools may pass into the exercise of skilled crafts and be saved from machine-minding. The skilled crafts or arts must be preserved, and some day we may wake up to find that the welfare of the nation depends on them.[1] I would have the educational bodies provide, as part of their scholarship programme, a few final Establishment-in-Business Bursaries for specially promising students in the technical schools. Never

[1] See *The Crafts and Reconstruction* (Arts and Crafts Society, 1919).

so small a wicket-gate leading out of the iron city of industrial toil would turn many faces hopefully in that direction, and it would be only an extension of the old and wise apprenticeship provisions.

Art in the life of the worker can only spring of hope and joy. When labour has been organized as an honoured national service, and when our towns have been made tidy and fit to live in, beauty will spring up of itself, and we shall not need any theory of art thrills, for beauty will be about us.

Chapter **XXI**

The Centre of Gravity [1]

A N old friend of mine used to say that the world, like a ship, had a wonderful self-righting power. We should all, I am sure, agree that a comparatively stable form of society depends like a ship on balance; and balance depends upon having the weighty things in the right place.

What is the first great necessity of Life? It is daily Labour. That is really all my little lecture, its text and theme. Work, as the first necessity of life, has to be recognized as the centre of gravity of the whole structure, and everything else in a sound and developing society should be seen in relation to productive work. Brainwork, sciences, fine-arts may all be noble and beneficial, but only so far as they are functions of the common society and part of a steady development of the great body of those who toil. Directly the brain-works go beyond this they are likely to become fevers and diseases in the social body. For instance, bombing is an amazing development of art and science, but it is a projection far from the centre of welfare. The answer is, I suppose, that while others do it so must we, but we are ourselves 'others' as well as 'we'. But all I am suggesting for the

[1] Summer School, Cambridge, 1920.

moment is that it would be well if 'science' had never found out the way. If science made a big gun that would blow the moon to bits some experimenter would feel justified in pulling the trigger. Further, while bombing flourishes housing must be neglected. We have not endless energy. It does not justify murder and robbery to call them science.

On looking back I see that I have always been puzzled to find myself in a world of people who had no teaching to give about living. I have found many curious separate spheres of thinking, whirling round, and grinding their own axes, but no general theory of ends and aims was discernible—only anxiety as to ways and means of going nowhere. Thus Political Economy called itself the science of wealth, but never attempted to say what wealth is; or if we accepted the assumption that it is profit, it has never set itself to explain 'what shall it profit' or what we should buy with it.

Education, too, has been conceived as concerned with 'knowledge', or sometimes as what the 'educated' called character—their knowledge and their character! This knowledge has for the most part become a knowledge of what is in print, an acquaintance with what may be said about things. Like economics, philosophy and theology, scholarship is largely a knowledge of stock answers, a method of out-arguing the other fellow, a way of scoring. Here I think I come near something fundamental to this age; our education from base to apex has very largely been a training in the art of scoring, a preparation for a professional career, a learning how to play cricket with words and football with lives.

We still live so near the origins of scholastic learning that we feel instinctively that there is a wizard mystery in writing and reading, and that people who can do it should be fattened at the public expense. It was well enough or no great harm, in the Middle Ages, that certain privileges should be granted to the little fringe of word-scholars, but obviously we can not all live by knowing names and writing: we can not all govern by giving posing or parliamentary answers: we can not all be fed by benefit of clergy: we may not always persuade the rest that work is low and that really good people must be protected from it. Just as we come to succeed the system will not work, for the rest will want to be good too!

Again, notice another subtlety of unconscious drift. For two or three hundred years, in fact ever since what has been called 'the revival of learning', there has been in process of development a method of skimming off a certain surface—the cream or grease—of work, and calling it by another name for the same thing, 'Art', thus to bribe 'artists' to separate from the great stock of which they are really only a part. This isolated art is all very well, but in truth, looking back on the exhibitions and press reviews, the collections and dispersals at Christie's, it is easy to see that it has been mainly regulated by dealers and provided as a background for financiers' dinner parties. When its history comes to be written it will doubtless be called dealer's art.

Labour, work, art, really make up what should be one body of human service, but 'fine art' has been trained to turn round and revile the rest for not being 'aesthetic'— whatever that may be—and then it gathers itself together in shilling bazaars for the annual amusement of country cousins in town.

It is really astounding, one of the unbelievable facts, that not only has it been bred into all the texture of our modern thinking that mere handiwork, doing things, being productive, and serving the world by labour is low, but our soul teachers have further seemed to suggest that work is wicked. They told us it was the 'curse'. They may say they found it so written, but hardly so. They were free to translate and stress and explain the dark old story as they liked, yet generations of people, since 'the revival of learning' especially, got the impression that labour was the curse. No wonder that all decent people and their teachers sought to be maintained remote from contact with anything so vile. The time has come, I am sure, for 'restatements', but pity 'tis they were not given before. If the world is to go on labour will have to be recognized by religion and philosophy. If any man would be a saint let him clean drains and dig the ground. Hidden in early Christian teaching are ideas which we never hear of now. One of these was the thought that the 'curse' was a blessing. It is probable, indeed, that the whole glorious unfolding of mediaeval art sprang from a thought of the heroism of labour, just as the expansion of the newspaper, now the news-manipulator, rests on the modern idea of the great glory of reading words in print.

I remember a beautiful sculptured sarcophagus of the fourth century. In the first panel was represented the Fall by eating the fruit of the Tree of Knowledge! In the next the Creator gave Adam a sheaf of corn and Eve a fleece for spinning. As the explanation of the illustration says, these were to be 'the instruments of their redemption'. In the celebrated early painted book, the Cotton Genesis, Adam and Eve are shown taking their digging and spinning implements with them out of Paradise—at least the blessed tools were holy things! Again, in the catacombs the tools of the crafts were so frequently represented that it is clear those who were buried had been proud of being producers. In one compartment which belonged to the guild of coopers there was a picture of them with their barrels—anything so real would be impossible in a modern church. It is significant, too, of the art of ancient Greece that Athene was the goddess of crafts—Athene the Worker. On the pedestal of her great gold and ivory image in the Parthenon Pheidias represented her giving a garment she had woven to the first woman, Pandora—the idea was the 'revelation' of the crafts to men.

Again, another most serious attack was made on honourable workmanship in the last century in the name of science, and people readily believed it, for 'science' was the favourite superstition of the time. This science under the specious title of political economy set to work to frame an apology for the violences of the industrial revolution, the tyranny of the great companies and the destruction of the beauty of our towns. The world-old traditions of noble workmanship were undermined, and gave way before the teaching of this new and true science of profit grinding and grabbing.

But even this was not all, there has been a tide in the affairs of men, and to crown and consummate nineteenth-century relations to workmanship came the organized ignorance called the Education Act of 1870, which turned

N*

the youth of the country from the practice of things into readers of print, leaving the print itself to be supplied by competitive publishers and the continuous journalism of the new press lords and viscounts.

It had to be: as those who could read and make curious black marks on paper claimed to be so different from the rest all at last had to be passed through one and the same mill. Probably, indeed, of course as it happened, it was inevitable; but if the world is to go on and up we shall (having acquired the print habit so that it can be naturally picked up in the home) have to educate for the proper works of life once more all over again.

If ever we are to remake civilization on a plan, we shall have to begin by recognizing that it is founded first of all on labour, without which it cannot last a day. We must understand and, as it is so mighty a necessity, we must even learn to worship work. We must learn to see in steady labourers the saints of Society. The ability to make is a form of culture as well as the ability to talk, and producing is really not less honourable than consuming. Even literary education itself has been far too much at war with creation, and the thoroughly educated literary person is such a fine and fragile flower that he is little likely to produce anything beyond critical and even cynical and corrosive opinions.

It is very disgusting to 'pure thought', but the first of propositions is that we live by daily eating. It is horrid to mention anything so vulgar, and such facts, like legs, are usually handsomely draped. That elegant exercise of high intelligences, 'philosophy', ignores the legs by cutting in on a superior plane: 'I think, therefore I am', it says, but this noble brainy structure will not march without legs. I eat, therefore I work, and I work, therefore I think, are necessary preliminaries. Now we are ready for a reasonable and not falsely refined life-philosophy—I eat, work, and think, therefore I am. As work is the first necessity of existence, the very centre of gravity of our moral system, so a proper recognition of work is a necessary basis for all right religion, art, and civilization. Society becomes diseased in direct ratio to its neglect and contempt of labour.

Chapter XXII

The Preservation of Ancient Architecture [1]

IN the course of the eighteenth and nineteenth centuries a great interest was developed in the ancient monuments of old lands, and the gradual and systematic study of ancient art has led to the perfecting of a second method of historical research, the history of Civilization by its monuments.

At the same time, while so much has been changing in the fashion of the world and of our lives, a conscious love of old works of art has been awakened in many minds, and a deep sentiment of communion with the men of the past through the works they have left to us has been aroused.

These, the historical and poetical aspects of old buildings are, it is self-evident, very largely dependent upon their authenticity as handed down from age to age. Such monuments, it must be realized, are not mere records, they are survivals, and a land in which they had been carefully conserved would carry on its past in actual being. We want not mere models and abstract shapes of buildings, but the very handiwork of the men of old, and the stones they laid. On the historical side, nothing else is a valid

[1] Architectural Conference, 1906.

document to be reasoned on, and, on the side of feeling and beauty, nothing else can really touch our imaginations.

While the branch of Archaeology dealing with the science of old building was being built up experts were naturally betrayed into mistakes by delight in their method of comparison and the consciousness of learning, by which they could see to some extent the completed form of fragmentary buildings; their mistakes, however, were manifold. They did not, in their eagerness, think of the difference between the mere imitation of an old monument (a model at full size, as it were, of what might have been) and the actual living building itself. They, as is well known, to bring the old and the new into 'harmony', often took away the oldness of the old part and made all new; and when they did not do this, they refused to see how they wounded the old by placing their office-made conjectures by the side of the actual works of art which they thought they were improving. It is impossible to tell of the involutions of error and confusion which have followed; the maddening contradictions of learned ignorance, of careful violence, of loving destruction, which have arisen in the application of the method.

Regrets for the past are vain, but in the present the charge, nay, the judgement, against restorers is that they are slow to learn. They acknowledge the irreparable harm that was done in the past, that was being done yesterday, and then, with all professions of understanding and sympathy, they go and do likewise; often, indeed, taking the new words, 'necessary repair', for the discredited old words, 'thorough restoration', with a very similar result.

Notwithstanding all the destruction wrought in the

last century, restoration is going forward at an accelerated rate all over Europe, and, of course, it is precisely the most ancient, remarkable, and beautiful buildings, which are laid hold of, passed through the mill of erudite restoration, and left desolate ghosts of themselves, ghosts to shudder at and pass on.

To tell of these things is too sadly absurd: of St. Front, at Périgeux, which excited so much interest in France that they made it over again with learned corrections: of Charlemagne's wonderful chapel at Aachen, a riddle which has never been read, where they are covering over the fine old masonry with fashionable marbles and mosaics like those in the smoking room of an hotel; and of Murano Cathedral, where the once mysterious and romantic apses now look as if they had been supplied from some cathedral factory in Chicago.

At San Vitale, Ravenna, astounding things have been going on for years under the direction of a learned scholar, but again it is the trivial, the obvious, and the vulgar which result from all this arrogance of learning. I say the trivial, and this may be illustrated by a point. Every one knows of the existence of a few wonderful old windows filled with sheets of translucent marble. The restorer simply cannot resist a chance like this of falling into a pitfall. Few and mysterious, are they? That is just what he wants, so with the help of a marble contractor he exploits them until they become a mere restorer's joke, and the Mausoleum of Galla Placidia looks like some grotto lit through yellow glass. The mosaics of St. Mark's, the West Front of Rheims, the porches of Chartres, the glass of Bourges, Chartres, and Sens—the great things of the world—all are being dealt with while we talk. As for England, I could tell many stories, but I know too much to trust myself.

In every country protests have been made. In France, Victor Hugo was stirred to passion by attacks on his Notre Dame, and lately a brilliant exposition of the method has been written by Emile Hovelacque. In Germany, Professor Strzygowski of Gratz has written an illuminating examination of the new splendours of the Dom of Aachen. In Italy, Cavalier Boni has criticized the restorations at Parenzo.

Thus, in one case, an Austrian Professor protests against what is done at Aachen, in the other, an Italian protests against the Austrians. I protest against the Italians and French, and invite any foreign member of this conference to protest against what we are doing in England, so as to complete a somewhat vicious circle of protestation, although undoubtedly each country has also had voices raised in its midst, as we have had Ruskin and Morris. But for the most part it must be said that everywhere the custodians of ancient buildings, and their architects, make a few verbal concessions and go smiling on their pre-destined way, while subscriptions obtained for urgent repairs are frequently transmuted into carvings and stained glass. In the recent report as to works said to be urgently required at St. Mark's, £5,000 is allocated to structural work and nearly £1,000 to decorative restorations, in-cluding a sum of £432 for further restorations of the Capitals, and proposals for restoring the pavement with-out estimate. As to these Capitals of St. Mark's, when in Venice I searched for three of the sixth century, which had on them monograms of the Emperor Justinian. It happened that all three had been cut out and replaced by exquisitely mechanical copies of fresh white marble, and I know of half a dozen sixth-century Capitals from St. Mark's in a private collection in London. None of us, I venture to say, could, without long research, say whether any of the old Capitals of the Ducal Palace are still in place.

What is the alternative to this now customary method of dealing with old buildings? It is persistent care and repair, as of national treasure to be guarded. Instead of the long intervals of neglect alternating with great 'restoration' campaigns, we need constant examination and minute reparations.

You have noticed some masterpieces in our Museums —the Venus of Milo at the Louvre, fragmentary sculptures from the Parthenon at the British Museum, the faded frescoes at the Brera—and felt that by the care taken of them they seemed all the more precious for showing a history of antiquity, loss, and disintegration. How precious must the armless Venus be which is set in such a place of honour in the greatest Museum in the world! Why are tiny pieces of red and black pottery brought from Greece and stuck together with such infinite pains, and placed so carefully in costly cases? They must surely have great historical value and beauty. So an old building, however much is lost, whatever be its state, should be cared for, in this spirit of proud guardianship; and then no necessary strengthening and upholding will harm it.

It is usual to object that old buildings are not in a Museum, and that they have to be maintained in use.

All the better, use would not hurt them. We must try to be honest there, and not let our pretences about use lead up to their bedizenment. The use and stability of our Cathedrals have again and again been sacrificed for the caprices of ornamental restoration, profuse in carvings, stained glass, and giant organs. Why should we call a building sacred as a preparation to making it a vulgar fraud? If the principle is accepted loyally that our object, while being guardians of a national or a world's treasure, is its integrity and obvious authenticity, we can hardly go wrong, and the horrors of restoration would fall away naturally. Time does not permit me to deal with detailed suggestions for the scientific protection of Ancient Buildings, but much experience is stored up in the printed matter issued by the Society I represent—the Society for the Protection of Ancient Buildings.

The great difficulty of the case is caused by the natural enthusiasm of the guardians and architects of old buildings for their own views about them. They have found out this and that—they believe that it was formerly so—and straightway they are anxious to make it so, not realizing that they cannot, and that even the theory is never certain. We know of the many supposed correct restorations which have been suggested on paper for the Parthenon and the Erechtheum, and of the continually shifting opinion on the evidence. Think of the confusion which has resulted from encouraging modern architects to *build* their theories of ancient buildings instead of embodying them in a tract, where they might be properly exposed and laughed at. In a treatise they could point to what actually remained, as evidence. In *building* their solid theories the evidence itself disappears, the validity of the old work is destroyed, and the whole becomes a monument of conjecture, a tantalizing mass of confusion which no one may read. They violently impose their ideas on old buildings, and we have not even the satisfaction of being able to show where they are wrong. Dead buildings tell no tales.

When I think of what is being done all over Europe, and being done now faster than at any other time, I am, indeed, filled with astonishment. It is almost impossible to visit any famous monument without finding it screened by scaffolding, and resounding with hammer strokes. I wonder here in England that it can still be done after all that has been said; I wonder in Italy that they do not realize that their ancient buildings give that country its pre-eminent value in the world; I wonder in France that their quick intelligence and artistic insight have not guided them in this question;—but most of all I think I wonder at the things which are being done in Germany, the land so justly famous for its historical criticism. Baedeker's guides to North and South Germany are hardly any longer indexes to old buildings so much as chronicles of restorations completed or in progress.

Unless this age of change and destruction is soon followed by one of anxious preservation there will be little left which is truly ancient to hand on to the Europe of the next generation.

Publisher's Notes to Second Edition

Pages

4   *The Dean's House, Wolverhampton:* demolished in 1931 and replaced by the Wolverhampton and Staffordshire Technical College.

17⎫ *Tube stations:* Lethaby's comments were made
84⎬ before the reconstruction of many London Under-
89⎭ ground stations; cf. Foreword to this edition, pp. xi–xii.

36   *L.C.C. Furniture School:* now the L.C.C. Technical College for the Furnishing Trades, Pitfield Street, Shoreditch, London, N.1.

49   *Waterloo Bridge:* the reference is to the bridge by John Rennie (1761–1821) opened in 1817; it was replaced by the present bridge designed by Sir Giles Gilbert Scott and opened in 1946.

70   *Wren:* Lethaby wrote before the founding of the Wren Society, which published between 1924 and 1943 twenty volumes reproducing Wren's original drawings, designs, and other material relating to his architectural work.

74   *Mr. James Bryce:* created Viscount Bryce in 1914.

Pages

118, fn. 2 ⎱ *Encyclopaedia Britannica:* the references are to
151   ⎰   the 11th edition (1910–11).

119   *Mr. A. J. Balfour:* created Earl of Balfour in 1922.

127   *Blastism:* i.e. the Vorticism publicized by Wynd-
      ham Lewis in his magazine *Blast* (1914–15).

140   *the elder Mr. Yeats:* John Butler Yeats (1839–1922)
      —usually known as Jack B. Yeats—painter;
      father of W. B. Yeats.

1957